AFRICAN WRITERS SERIES

PETER ABRAHAMS
6 *Mine Boy*

CHINUA ACHEBE
1 *Things Fall Apart*
3 *No Longer at Ease*
16 *Arrow of God*
31 *A Man of the People*
100 *Girls at War*•
120 *Beware Soul Brother*†

THOMAS AKARE
241 *The Slums*

TEWFIK AL-HAKIM
117 *The Fate of a Cockroach*‡

T. M. ALUKO
11 *One Man, One Matchet*
30 *One Man, One Wife*
32 *Kinsman and Foreman*
70 *Chief, the Honourable Minister*
130 *His Worshipful Majesty*
242 *Wrong Ones in the Dock*

ELECHI AMADI
25 *The Concubine*
44 *The Great Ponds*
140 *Sunset in Biafra*§
210 *The Slave*

JARED ANGIRA
111 *Silent Voices*†

I. N. C. ANIEBO
148 *The Anonymity of Sacrifice*
206 *The Journey Within*
253 *Of Wives, Talismans and the Dead*•

KOFI ANYIDOHO
261 *A Harvest of Our Dreams*†

AYI KWEI ARMAH
43 *The Beautyful Ones Are Not Yet Born*
154 *Fragments*
155 *Why Are We So Blest?*
194 *The Healers*
218 *Two Thousand Seasons*

BEDIAKO ASARE
59 *Rebel*

KOFI AWOONOR
108 *This Earth, My Brother*
260 *Until the Morning After*†

MARIAMA BÂ
248 *So Long a Letter*

FRANCIS BEBEY
205 *The Ashanti Doll*

MONGO BETI
13 *Mission to Kala*
77 *King Lazarus*
88 *The Poor Christ of Bomba*
181 *Perpetua and the Habit of Unhappiness*
214 *Remember Ruben*

STEVE BIKO
217 *I Write What I Like*§

OKOT P'BITEK
147 *The Horn of My Love*†
193 *Hare and Hornbill*•
266 *Song of Lawino & Song of Ocol*†

YAW M. BOATENG
186 *The Return*

Novels
•Short S
†Poetry
‡Plays
§Biogra

DENNIS
46 *Lett*
115 *A Si*
208 *Stub*

AMILCAR CABRAL
198 *Unity and Struggle*§

SYL CHENEY-COKER
221 *The Graveyard Also Has Teeth*†

DRISS CHRAIBI
79 *Heirs to the Past*

J. P. CLARK
50 *America, Their America*§

WILLIAM CONTON
12 *The African*

BERNARD B. DADIE
87 *Climbié*

DANIACHEW WORKU
125 *The Thirteenth Sun*

MODIKWE DIKOBE
124 *The Marabi Dance*

DAVID DIOP
174 *Hammer Blows*†

MBELLA SONNE DIPOKO
57 *Because of Women*
82 *A Few Nights and Days*
107 *Black and White in Love*†

AMU DJOLETO
41 *The Strange Man*
161 *Money Galore*

T. OBINKARAM ECHEWA
168 *The Land's Lord*

CYPRIAN EKWENSI
2 *Burning Grass*
5 *People of the City*
19 *Lokotown*•
84 *Beautiful Feathers*
146 *Jagua Nana*
172 *Restless City*•
185 *Survive the Peace*

BUCHI EMECHETA
227 *The Joys of Motherhood*

OLAUDAH EQUIANO
10 *Equiano's Travels*§

MALICK FALL
144 *The Wound*

NURUDDIN FARAH
80 *From a Crooked Rib*
184 *A Naked Needle*
226 *Sweet and Sour Milk*
252 *Sardines*

MUGO GATHERU
20 *Child of Two Worlds*§

FATHY GHANEM
223 *The Man Who Lost His Shadow*

NADINE GORDIMER
177 *Some Monday for Sure*•

JOE DE GRAFT
166 *Beneath the Jazz and Brass*†
264 *Muntu*‡

An Egyptian Childhood

YUSUF IDRIS
209 *The Cheapest Nights*•
267 *Rings of Burnished Brass*•

OBOTUNDE IJIMÈRE
18 *The Imprisonment of Obatala*‡

EDDIE IROH
189 *Forty-Eight Guns for the General*
213 *Toads of War*
255 *The Siren in the Night*

KENJO JUMBAM
231 *The White Man of God*

AUBREY KACHINGWE
24 *No Easy Task*

SAMUEL KAHIGA
158 *The Girl from Abroad*

CHEIKH HAMIDOU KANE
119 *Ambiguous Adventure*

KENNETH KAUNDA
4 *Zambia Shall Be Free*§

LEGSON KAYIRA
162 *The Detainee*

A. W. KAYPER-MENSAH
157 *The Drummer in Our Time*†

JOMO KENYATTA
219 *Facing Mount Kenya*§

ASARE KONADU
40 *A Woman in her Prime*
55 *Ordained by the Oracle*

AHMADOU KOUROUMA
239 *The Suns of Independence*

MAZISI KUNENE
211 *Emperor Shaka the Great*†
234 *Anthem of the Decades*†
235 *The Ancestors*†

ALEX LA GUMA
35 *A Walk in the Night*•
110 *In the Fog of the Seasons' End*
152 *The Stone Country*
212 *Time of the Butcherbird*

DORIS LESSING
131 *The Grass is Singing*

HUGH LEWIN
251 *Bandiet*

TABAN LO LIYONG
69 *Fixions*•
74 *Eating Chiefs*•
90 *Frantz Fanon's Uneven Ribs*†
116 *Another Nigger Dead*†

BONNIE LUBEGA
105 *The Outcasts*

YULISA AMADU MADDY
89 *Obasai*‡
137 *No Past, No Present, No Future*

NAGUIB MAHFOUZ
197 *Miramar*
225 *Children of Gebelawi*
NELSON MANDELA
123 *No Easy Walk to Freedom*§
JACK MAPANJE
236 *Of Chameleons and Gods*†
DAMBUDZO MARECHERA
207 *The House of Hunger**
237 *Black Sunlight*
ALI A. MAZRUI
97 *The Trial of Christopher Okigbo*
TOM MBOYA
81 *The Challenge of Nationhood (Speeches)*§
S. O. MEZU
113 *Behind the Rising Sun*
THOMAS MOFOLO
229 *Chaka*
HAM MUKASA
133 *Sir Apolo Kagwa Discovers Britain*§
DOMINIC MULAISHO
98 *The Tongue of the Dumb*
204 *The Smoke that Thunders*
CHARLES L. MUNGOSHI
170 *Waiting for the Rain*
JOHN MUNONYE
21 *The Only Son*
45 *Obi*
94 *Oil Man of Obange*
153 *A Dancer of Fortune*
195 *Bridge to a Wedding*
MARTHA MVUNGI
159 *Three Solid Stones**
MEJA MWANGI
143 *Kill Me Quick*
145 *Carcase for Hounds*
176 *Going Down River Road*
GEORGE SIMEON MWASE
160 *Strike a Blow and Die*§
JOHN NAGENDA
262 *The Seasons of Thomas Tebo*
NGUGI WA THIONG'O
7 *Weep Not, Child*
17 *The River Between*
36 *A Grain of Wheat*
51 *The Black Hermit*‡
150 *Secret Lives**
188 *Petals of Blood*
200 *Devil on the Cross*
240 *Detained*§
NGUGI & MICERE MUGO
191 *The Trial of Dedan Kimathi*‡
NGUGI & NGUGI WA MIRII
246 *I Will Marry When I Want*‡
REBEKA NJAU
203 *Ripples in the Pool*
ARTHUR NORTJE
141 *Dead Roots*†
NKEM NWANKWO
67 *Danda*
173 *My Mercedes is Bigger Than Yours*
FLORA NWAPA
26 *Efuru*
56 *Idu*

S. NYAMFUKUDZA
233 *The Non-Believer's Journey*
ONUORA NZEKWU
85 *Wand of Noble Wood*
91 *Blade Among the Boys*
OLUSEGUN OBASANJO
249 *My Command*§
OGINGA ODINGA
38 *Not Yet Uhuru*§
GABRIEL OKARA
68 *The Voice*
183 *The Fisherman's Invocation*†
CHRISTOPHER OKIGBO
62 *Labyrinths*†
KOLE OMOTOSO
102 *The Edifice*
122 *The Combat*
SEMBENE OUSMANE
63 *God's Bits of Wood*
92 *The Money-Order*
175 *Xala*
250 *The Last of the Empire*
YAMBO OUOLOGUEM
99 *Bound to Violence*
MARTIN OWUSU
138 *The Sudden Return*‡
FERDINAND OYONO
29 *Houseboy*
39 *The Old Man and the Medal*
PETER K. PALANGYO
53 *Dying in the Sun*
SOL T. PLAATJE
201 *Mhudi*
PEPETELA
269 *Mayombe*
R. L. PETENI
178 *Hill of Fools*
LENRIE PETERS
22 *The Second Round*
37 *Satellites*†
238 *Selected Poetry*†
MOLEFE PHETO
258 *And Night Fell*§
J.-J. RABEARIVELO
167 *Translations from the Night*†
MUKOTANI RUGYENDO
187 *The Barbed Wire*
MWANGI RUHENI
139 *The Future Leaders*
156 *The Minister's Daughter*
TAYEB SALIH
47 *The Wedding of Zein**
66 *Season of Migration to the North*
STANLAKE SAMKANGE
33 *On Trial for my Country*
169 *The Mourned One*
190 *Year of the Uprising*
WILLIAMS SASSINE
199 *Wirriyamu*
KOBINA SEKYI
136 *The Blinkards*‡
SAHLE SELLASSIE
163 *Warrior King*
FRANCIS SELORMEY
27 *The Narrow Path*
L. S. SENGHOR
71 *Nocturnes*†
180 *Prose and Poetry*
SIPHO SEPAMLA
268 *A Ride on the Whirlwind*

MONGANE SEROTE
263 *To Every Birth Its Blood*
ROBERT SERUMAGA
54 *Return to the Shadows*
WOLE SOYINKA
76 *The Interpreters*
TCHICAYA U TAM'SI
72 *Selected Poems*†
CAN THEMBA
104 *The Will to Die**
REMS NNA UMEASIEGBU
61 *The Way We Lived**
LAWRENCE VAMBE
112 *An Ill-Fated People*§
J. L. VIEIRA
202 *The Real Life of Domingos Xavier*
222 *Luuanda*
JOHN YA-OTTO
244 *Battlefront Namibia*§
ASIEDU YIRENKYI
216 *Kivuli and Other Plays*‡
D. M. ZWELONKE
128 *Robben Island*
COLLECTIONS OF PROSE
9 *Modern African Prose*
14 *Quartet*
23 *The Origin of Life and Death*
48 *Not Even God is Ripe Enough*
58 *Political Spider*
75 *Myths and Legends of the Swahili*
83 *Myths and Legends of the Congo*
109 *Onitsha Market Literature*
118 *Amadu's Bundle*
132 *Two Centuries of African English*
192 *Egyptian Short Stories*
243 *Africa South Contemporary Writings*
254 *Stories from Central and Southern Africa*
256 *Unwinding Threads*
259 *This is the Time*
270 *African Short Stories*
ANTHOLOGIES OF POETRY
8 *A Book of African Verse*
42 *Messages: Poems from Ghana*
64 *Seven South African Poets*
93 *A Choice of Flowers*
96 *Poems from East Africa*
106 *French African Verse*
129 *Igbo Traditional Verse*
164 *Black Poets in South Africa*
171 *Poems of Black Africa*
192 *Anthology of Swahili Poetry*
215 *Poems from Angola*
230 *Poets to the People*
257 *New Poetry from Africa*
COLLECTIONS OF PLAYS
28 *Short East African Plays*
34 *Ten One-Act Plays*
78 *Short African Plays*
114 *Five African Plays*
127 *Nine African Plays for Radio*
134 *African Theatre*
165 *African Plays for Playing 1*
179 *African Plays for Playing 2*
224 *South African People's Plays*
232 *Egyptian One-Act Plays*

A New Book of AFRICAN VERSE

compiled and edited by

JOHN REED & CLIVE WAKE

HEINEMANN
LONDON · IBADAN · NAIROBI

Heinemann Educational Books Ltd
22 Bedford Square, London WC1B 3HH
PMB 5205, Ibadan. PO Box 45314, Nairobi

EDINBURGH MELBOURNE AUCKLAND
HONG KONG SINGAPORE KUALA LUMPUR
NEW DELHI KINGSTON PORT OF SPAIN

First published as *A Book of African Verse* 1964
This revised edition 1984

British Library Cataloguing in Publication Data

A New book of African verse.—Revised ed.
—(African writers series; 8)
1. African poetry (English)
I. Reed, John, *1929–* II. Wake, Clive III. A
Book of African verse IV. Series
821'.008'096 PR9346

ISBN 0–435–90308–X

Set in 10pt Garamond by Performance Typesetters, Milton Keynes
Printed in Great Britain by Richard Clay (The Chaucer Press) Ltd,
Bungay, Suffolk

Contents

Acknowledgements

The editors and publisher would like to thank the following for permission to reproduce copyright material:

Ama Ata Aidoo for 'From the only speech that was not delivered at the Rally', **John Pepper Clark** for 'You May Well Cry' from *The Song of a Goat*, 'Night Rain', 'Ibadan', 'Incident at the Police Station, Warri', 'The Casualties' and 'The Lagos-Ibadan Road before Shagamu'; **Rex Collings**, London for 'The Island', 'Words, Words, Words' and 'In Search of Roots' by Sipho Sepamla from *The Soweto I Love* and 'Telephone Conversation', 'Three Millet Stalks' and 'To the Madmen Over the Wall' by Wole Soyinka; **Andre Deutsch**, London for 'Place of Dreams' and 'The Gold-miners' by Mazisi Kunene from *Zulu Poems*; **Ad. Donker**, Johannesburg for 'One Small Boy Longs for Summer' by Pascal Mafika Gwala from *Jol'inkomo*, 'A Newly-born Calf', 'Pigeons at the Oppenheimer Park', 'A Brazier in the Street', 'Sunset', 'The Face of Hunger' and 'Amagoduka at Glencoe Station' by Oswald Mtshali from *Sounds of a Cowhide Drum*, 'The Loneliness Beyond' by Sipho Sepamla from *Hurry Up To It*, 'A Ballad of the Thing' by Sipho Sepamla from *The Blues is You in Me*, 'For Don M. – Banned' by Mongane Wally Serote from *Tsetlo*, 'Ofay-watcher, Throbs-phase' by Mongane Wally Serote from *Yakhal'inkomo*, 'I Can Say' by Mongane Wally Serote from *No Baby Must Weep* and 'When Lights Go Out' by Mongane Wally Serote from *Behold Mama, Flowers*; **East African Publishing House**, Nairobi for extracts by Okot p'Bitek from *The Song of Lawino*; **Editions Pierre Jean Oswald**, Paris for 'A Woman Speaks' by Jean-Baptiste Tati-Loutard from *Les Racines congolaises*, 'Backside of the Sun', 'Return from Ethiopia' and 'Crisis of Faith at St. Anne's' by Jean-Baptiste Tati-Loutard from *L'Envers du soleil*, 'Symbol' by Tchicaya U Tam'si from *Le Mauvais Sang* and 'Rape' by Tchicaya U Tam'si from *L'Arc musical*; **Editions Robert Laffont**, Paris for 'The Lines of Our Hands' and 'Leaf in the Wind' by Bernard B. Dadie and 'You Will Walk in Peace' by Martial Sinda; **Editions du Seuil**, Paris for 'All Day Long', 'Taga for Mbaye Dyob', 'Ndesse', 'To the American Negro Soldiers', 'Message', 'Your Letter on the Sheet' and 'And the Sun' by Leopold Sedar Senghor; **Heinemann Educational Books**, London for 'Rediscovery' by Kofi Awoonor from *A Book of African Verse*, 'The Place' and 'One Along: The Bird Sweeps' (extract from 'The Wayfarer Comes Home') by

Kofi Awoonor from *Until the Morning After*, 'On the Island', 'Steeling Oneself to Face the Day' and 'In the Dove-Grey Dove-Soft Dusk' by Dennis Brutus from *A Simple Lust*, 'It Was a Sherded World I Entered', 'They Hanged Him, I Said Dismissively' and 'Robben Island Sequence' by Dennis Brutus from *Stubborn Hope*, 'Looking for the Spirit at Night' by Syl Cheney-Coker from *The Graveyard Also Has Teeth*, 'The Rock Behind the Fort' by Joe de Graft from *Beneath the Jazz and Brass*, 'Autobiography' and 'My Brother and I Left the Apartment' (extract from 'The Return from Tangier') by Mbella Sonne Dipoko from *Black and White in Love*, 'A Heritage of Liberation', 'Sword Eulogizing Itself After a Massacre', 'The Fearful Ruins', 'The Great Ones' and 'In Praise of the Ancestors' by Mazisi Kunene from *The Ancestors & the Sacred Mountain*, 'Song from the Congolese' by Taban lo Liyong from *Franz Fanon's Uneven Ribs*, 'Song for a Passport', 'Letter from Pretoria Central Prison', 'Native's Letter', 'Untitled' and 'All Hungers Pass Away' by Arthur Nortje from *Dead Roots*, 'For Georgette', 'Come Thunder', 'Hurrah for Thunder' and 'Elegy for Alto' by Christopher Okigbo from *Labyrinths* and 'Parachute', 'You Talk to Me of "Self"' and 'What Do You Do' by Lenrie Peters from *Selected Poetry*; **Heinemann Educational Books**, London and **Ethiope Publishing Corporation**, Benin City for 'You Laughed and Laughed and Laughed' and 'One Night at Victoria Beach' by Gabriel Okara from *The Fisherman's Invocation*; **Bernard Kojo Laing** for 'Jazz Song', 'Bring It Here' and 'Miles: Poem on a Runway'; **Libraria Sa Da Costa Editora**, Lisbon for 'Between' (Pausa), 'Night' (Noite), 'Don't Ask Me For Smiles' (Nao me pecas sorrisos) and 'Kinaxixi' by Agostinho Neto from *Sagrada esperanca*; Methuen, London for 'Koko Oloro' by Wole Soyinka from *Idanre and Other Poems*; **Les Nouvelles Editions Africaines**, Dakar for 'Speech Was Bequeathed Me' and 'Master of the Initiates' by Fernando d'Almeida from *Traduit de je pluriel*; **Gabriel Okara** for 'Were I to Choose' and **Presence Africaine**, Paris for 'Viaticum' and 'Breath' by Birago Diop from *Leurres et lueurs*, 'Waves', 'Defiance Against Force', 'Times' and 'Africa' by David Diop from *Coups de pilon*, 'Schoolboys' and 'Empty Heads' by Malick Fall from *Reliefs*, 'Tomatoes' by Yambo Ouologuem and 'I Could Say' by Tchicaya U Tam'si from *Le Ventre/Le Pain ou la cendre*.

Introduction

The present volume is a new and revised edition of *A Book of African Verse* as first published in the African Writers Series in 1964. In making this revision we have omitted thirty-three poems that were published in the first version, amounting to some 1,700 lines, and added seventy-nine poems or passages from poems not included in that volume, amounting to some 2,400 lines. In the introduction which we wrote twenty years ago we remarked; 'All the poetry in this book belongs to the last thirty years and much of it is written by poets who are still young'. In fact the great majority of the poems, at least of those written in English, had been written in the last decade. In the time that has passed since then, the young poets of 1964 have reached maturity and a new generation of poets has appeared. African writing has become an accepted subject of study in schools and universities, with its own critical literature and its own fierce controversies. Certainly the experience of anthologizing has been different. In the early sixties, apart from one or two established names in French African poetry, our task was to seek out poems where they could be found – mostly in journals and small locally printed collections. In the early eighties, the task has been the bulk of reading and rereading to be done in the many collections of poetry published by Africans in England, France and in the African countries and the problem has been to make a selection which would be representative of the best work and yet could be fitted into a fairly small volume.

A Book of African Verse was particularly intended for readers coming to African poetry – understood as poetry written by Africans in English together with some translations of poems written by Africans in French – for the first time. In 1964 almost all potential readers fell into this group. The fact that the book has continued in demand in the changed circumstances of the rise of African literature and the appearance of other, more recent and extensive anthologies, suggests it has found a place as a first anthology and an introduction to contemporary poetry in schools in Africa. In revising the volume therefore we have to keep in mind that original intention of providing an introduction to new readers of African poetry.

The scope of the book is given in the opening paragraph of the original introduction:

This book gives a selection of the poetry written by Africans in English, together with some translations into English of poems written by Africans in

French. It is not an anthology drawn from the whole field of African poetry. It does not represent the traditional poetry of Africa's many vernacular languages, nor does it represent the poetry which is today growing up side by side with the traditional poetry, the work of modern African poets who write and publish their poetry instead of reciting it and who are often influenced by European poetry, but who continue to use their own vernacular languages. Whether the future of African poetry lies mainly with this vernacular poetry or whether it lies in the development of an African tradition in French poetry and English poetry we do not know. But for many years it is probable that some African poets will continue writing in the African languages, and some in the main European languages which are used in Africa for administration, education and international purposes.

Nothing here needs revising, except to add 'Portuguese' to the references to English and French – since it seemed we ought to include some poems by the distinguished Angolan poet, Agostinho Neto. It is still far too early to know how African culture will in the long run make use of the various languages which are available to it. For the time being English, French and Portuguese continue to be used by some of the continent's poets.

Our method in bringing the anthology up to date has been to read as much as we could discover of the verse which has appeared since we completed the first anthology and to select from this. When we have included later work of the poets who appeared in the first version we have in almost every case retained all the poems we gave in 1964. Although the new version is longer, it has been necessary to leave out some poems included before. These have been the poems we felt we would not have put in if we had been making the anthology for the first time today. Some of these poems will be missed, particularly perhaps James Jolobe's long narrative poem *Thuthula.* In the first collection, Jolobe was our only poet from South Africa. The remarkable constellation of poets which arose in that country in the seventies has, we feel, properly taken its place in the new version. In the interests of space we have also excluded the Malagasy poets we gave in 1964, adopting the stricter interpretation of the limits of African literature which is now usual.

Inevitably with the much richer field from which to choose, a larger element of purely personal choice and preference has entered into our selection. If our taste has led us more towards poems of experience and observation than to those of philosophical consideration or political declaration, more towards a poetry of direct utterance than of allusion and elaboration, this also seemed to be the most suitable poetry to serve as an introduction to new readers. We have tried to bring in as much variety as possible both in form and content rather than to confine ourselves in each poet to the most ambitious or most typical poems. We have retained the lay-out of the first *Book of African Verse,* the alphabetical arrangement by author's name and the brief notes on some of the poems. We have added a brief guide to other collections of African verse, both general and specialized.

AMA ATA AIDOO

Born in 1942 near Dominasa, Ghana. She has a well-established reputation as a playwright and short-story writer.

From the Only Speech That Was Not Delivered At the Rally

Amanfuo,
just look at
us
                and
know
the full
extent of
your distress.

Between me
                    and   10
the other candidate,
there's quite a lot to choose from:

an extra inch or so of
bones,
a few pounds' difference –
in weight.

Where one was born is
most important. Especially when
we
tell   20
you
so.

Do take note
                                        and
not forget
to give me your vote
along with your
                                                  wife.

I am your tribesman:
                                                  and   30
who else but I,
your own housefly,
can suck your
                                                  wounds
to hurt the most?

Education too
must not be missed.

                                                  Or
how could we who have the best
make you and them   40
who have the least
or none at all
look small?

For the rest, dear countrymen,
we promise you
no success
no prosperity.

Man must have something to live for.

We survive on our
failures.   50

As things
do stand,
I've missed more
chances

than
I can count,
or
wish to count.

So
Time gives 60
Me her
'Go-ahead'
to chop you small
before I'm dead.

FERNANDO D'ALMEIDA

Born in 1955 of parents from two different African countries: Benin (formerly Dahomey) and Cameroon. He lives in Cameroon, where he works as a journalist. He has published two books of poetry: *Au seuil de l'exil* (P.J. Oswald, 1976); *Traduit du je pluriel* (Nouvelles Editions Africaines, 1980).

Speech Was Bequeathed Me

Speech was bequeathed me
to lower the mask of lies
Speech was given me
to share in the mating season of my people

I am outside to impose on the heedless
the inaugural lecture of exigency
To revise my childhood
like a schoolboy revising his algebra

I begin – with the help of time –
to understand why I have no respite from pleading 10
From wanting to tell all beneath the tires of writing
I begin to see myself apart from the hesitant

To live better
I ask that from the flux of language
My people carry me on their long crutches
that, ripening the work of my life,
I may set myself up in the poem of fervour

For, before going to the spring of day to draw
the eternal themes of poetry,
It behoves that in this night snared with contradictions 20
I make a pact with upright men
That my speech may attain the sea-marks of Knowledge

Translated from the French

Master of the Initiates

Master of the Initiates
I am here invited to the sanctuary of Learning
I have cut my nails and shaved my hair
I come to you impelled by the word of the poem
To speak with you in images after the fashion of dreaming men
Who fling themselves into action to give their lives a sense
I have watched all night to spy the day
On the outskirts of essential speech
I have watched at the votive altar of the gods
That, husking the words of ritual, 10
I may come to the Knowledge which is the source of love

Translated from the French

KOFI AWOONOR

Born in 1935 at Wheta, in the Volta region of Ghana. He studied in Ghana, Britain and the United States and has taught in universities in Ghana and the United States. He has been on the editorial committee of *Okyeame.* He is co-editor of *Messages: Poems from Ghana* (1971) and the author of a novel and plays, and he has published several volumes of poetry: *Rediscovery and other poems* (Mbari, 1964); *Night of My Blood*

(Doubleday, 1971); *Ride Me, Memory* (Greenfield Review Press, 1973); *The House by the Sea* (Greenfield Review Press, 1978). His collected poems will be published by Heinemann (African Writers Series) in 1985.

Rediscovery

When our tears are dry on the shore
and the fishermen carry their nets home
and the seagulls return to bird island
and the laughter of children recedes at night
there shall still linger the communion we forged
the feast of oneness whose ritual we partook of
There shall still be the eternal gateman
who will close the cemetery doors
and send the late mourners away
It cannot be the music we heard that night 10
that still lingers in the chambers of memory
It is the new chorus of our forgotten comrades
and the halleluyahs of our second selves

The Place

You remember sometimes
that the place is by the sea,
And once in a while you see a gull
rise
swift against the blazing sun
in dazzling colours playing
in the shards of a noonday.
It's always so swift, so brief
At night you recall it all
while the door is locked. 10

One Alone: The Bird Sweeps

(from *The Wayfarer Comes Home)*

At the first journey, at dawn
the sea emerges. Some call her mad
She yields to the land of pure sand
beautiful beyond recalling.
On clear days, the eye
can sweep across the old plantation
maintained once by slave labour
its harvest long buried in history
the grandeur of this land
defies poetry and music 10
But they still sing of her
in long voluminous poems
in elaborate symphonies
There is rhythm of course
as you cannot talk
of this land without rhythm.

Evening is the time for fires
the cowherds driving their wards across the grassland
fishermen sharing the last catch;
each gesture a caress, an embrace 20
of this lover land.
The long last light bursts
upon the houses made of branches,
the light wind steadies the flicker
of the oil lamps
as they burn in the naked twilight.

Beyond this lies deep penetration of forests
home for gnomic tendencies
and tribal mysteries;
they embrace mountains and hills 30
    we call them mountains for we love them
    circular immense yet fragile
    splendid like pubertal dances.

They state the reality of love
the claims of kinship
They too sing their dark jubilee
near forgotten villages
longing for the abundant time.

What can I say of you now
You whose mystery keeps me in hope 40
intangible cause that depicts the effect,
the love that put me to sea?
What can I say of you now?
You state the wizardry of my loins
The certainty of my despair,
My heart clothed in a torn jumper
leaps to be delivered
from this ineffable pain

Mother, mother, my mother
the hearth is cold 50
the house is empty
the people are all gone

But I raise up now
the dying animal of love.
The sun proclaims me a claimant
to an ancient stool
releases me from all foreign vows.
The wind the sea and the forest stress
the proclamation of the rain
and the light enunciates 60
the inexorable tenderness
I love you, I love you
tatters and all. I shield you
with my pain.
I seek release from diseases
so I can bring you cure.
Take away this fatigue of the soul,
send a message to Soweto
on my behalf.

Tell them the festival time is come 70
that the heap slags of the raw cities
will burn,
that the dance has begun
the drummers all in place;
this dreary half life is over
our dream will be born at noon.
The night is for plots and stratagems.
We shall harness the flames for the revolt
pride shall lead us into armouries

We shall stalk the evil animal 80
        a hundred years times ten hundred
        even beyond the moon.
We abjure all malice
We claim the sanctity of the ambush
        and clean revenge.
We love the smell of dead animals.

In this hour before victory
trace me every line on the dragonfly
count me the legs of the spider hen
the various tongues of water 90
        and the criss cross of the wind.
Tell me how often the baboon fornicates
how frequent the mountains breathe.
The fish says I know his hiding place
Already the gull's island is my treasure store
Gemi and Amu, mountain and river
shift the stress upon my heart.

So I make this journey now;
there will be no detours
I shall live on rawhide and locusts 100
I shall drink of the only wine you serve
        and in the ugly hour long ordained
I shall grind my knife.

I will have no trophies to show
For the swamp beneath the hills
shall receive the evil animal.

DENNIS BRUTUS

Born in 1924 in Salisbury, Southern Rhodesia (Zimbabwe). Brought up in South Africa where he completed his university studies and taught before leaving in 1966. He is president of SANROC (South African Non-racial Olympic Committee) and has worked with the International Defence and Aid Fund. He has travelled widely and taught in the United States. He has published several volumes of poetry: *Sirens, Knuckles and Boots* (Mbari, 1963); *Letters to Martha* (Heinemann, 1968); *Poems from Algiers* (University of Texas, 1970); *A Simple Lust* – a substantial selection from these three volumes (Heinemann, 1973); *Stubborn Hope* (Heinemann, 1978).

On the Island

I

Cement-grey floors and walls
cement-grey days
cement-grey time
and a grey susurration
as of seas breaking
winds blowing
and rains drizzling.

A barred existence
so that one did not need to look
at doors or windows 10
to know that they were sundered by bars
and one locked in a grey gelid stream
of unmoving time.

II

When the rain came
it came in a quick moving squall
moving across the island
murmuring from afar
then drumming on the roof
then marching fading away.

And sometimes one mistook 20
the weary tramp of feet
as the men came shuffling from the quarry
white-dust-filmed and shambling
for the rain
that came and drummed and marched away.

III

It was not quite envy
nor impatience
nor irritation
but a mixture of feelings
one felt 30
for the aloof deep-green dreaming firs
that poised in the island air
withdrawn, composed and still.

IV

On Saturday afternoons we were embalmed in time
like specimen moths pressed under glass;
we were immobile in the sunlit afternoon
waiting;
Visiting time:
until suddenly like a book snapped shut
all possibilities vanished as zero hour passed 40
and we knew another week would have to pass.

Steeling Oneself to Face the Day

Steeling oneself to face the day
girding one's self for the wrap of clothes
bracing oneself for the thrust of the world
one buckles to buttons and zips and belts:
With the gritted reluctance and indifference to pain
with which one enters an unsought fight
one accepts the challenge the bullying day thrusts down.

In the Dove-Grey Dove-Soft Dusk

In the dove-grey dove-soft dusk
when the walls softened to frozen smoke
and their rigidity melted
receding to miles,
when the air was alive and tender
with a mist of spray from the sea,
the air luminous
and the sky bright with the dulling glimmer
of cooling molten lead;
when the island breathed – 10
trees, grass, stones and sand breathing
quietly at the end of the long hot day –
and the sea was a soft circling presence –
no longer a tight barbed menacing ring:
in the dusk
nothing was more agonizing than to be seized
by the poignant urgent simple desire
simply to stroll in the quiet dusk:
as I do now:
as I do now, and they do not. 20

It Was a Sherded World I Entered

It was a sherded world I entered:
of broken bottles, rusty tins and split rooftiles:
the littered earth was full of menace
with jagged edges waiting the naked feet:
holes, trenches, ditches were scattered traps
and the broken land in wasteplots our playing field:
this was the world through which I learnt the world
and this the image for my vision of the world.

They Hanged Him, I Said Dismissively

They hanged him, I said dismissively
having no other way to say he died
or that he was a dear friend
or that work wove us most intimately
in common tasks, ambitions, desires.
Now he is dead: and I dare not think
of the anguish that drove him to where he was
or the pain at their hands he must have faced
or how much he was racked by my distress:
now, it is still easiest to say, they hanged him, 10
dismissively.

Robben Island Sequence

I

neonbright orange
vermilion
on the chopped broken slate
that gravelled the path and yard
bright orange was the red blood
freshly spilt where the prisoners had passed;

and bright red
pinkbright red and light
the blood on the light sand by the sea
the pale lightyellow seas and 10
in the light bright airy air
lightwoven, seawoven, spraywoven air
of sunlight by the beach where we worked:

where the bright blade-edges of the rocks
jutted like chisels from the squatting rocks
the keen fine edges whitening to thinness
from the lightbrown masses of the sunlit rocks,
washed around by swirls on rushing wave water,
lightgreen or colourless, transparent with a hint of light:

on the sharp pale whitening edges 20
our blood showed light and pink,
our gashed soles winced from the fine barely felt slashes,
that lacerated afterwards:
the bloody flow
thinned to thin pink strings dangling
as we hobbled through the wet clinging sands
or we discovered surprised
in some quiet backwater pool
the thick flow of blood uncoiling
from a skein to thick dark red strands. 30

The menace of that bright day was clear as the blade of a knife;
from the blade edges of the rocks,
from the piercing brilliance of the day,
the incisive thrust of the clear air into the lungs
the salt-stinging brightness of sky and light on the eyes:
from the clear image, bronze-sharp lines of Kleynhans laughing
khaki-ed, uniformed, with his foot on the neck of the convict
who had fallen,
holding his head under water in the pool where he had fallen
while the man thrashed helplessly
and the bubbles gurgled 40
and the air glinted dully on lethal gunbutts,
the day was brilliant with the threat of death.

II

sitting on the damp sand
in sand-powdered windpuff,
the treetops still grey in the early morning air
and dew still hanging tree-high,
to come to the beginning of the day
and small barely-conscious illicit greetings
to settle to a shape of mind, of thought,
and inhabit a body to its extremities: 50
to be a prisoner, a political victim,
to be a some-time fighter, to endure –
find reserves of good cheer, of composure
while the wind rippled the tight skin forming on the cooling porridge
and sandspray dropped by windgusts depressed it:
to begin, at the beginning of a day, to be a person
and take and hold a shape to last for this one day . . .

(afterwards the old lags came along
with their favourite warders, to select
the young prisoners who had caught their eye, 60
so that these could be assigned to their span)

III

some mornings we lined up for 'hospital'
– it meant mostly getting castor oil –
but what a varied bunch we were!
for all had injuries – but in such variety
split heads; smashed ankles, arms;
cut feet in bandages, or torn and bloodied legs:
some, under uniform, wore their mass of bruises
but what a bruised and broken motley lot we were!

SYL CHENEY-COKER

Born in 1945 in Freetown, Sierra Leone. He studied at universities in the United States and worked as a journalist before becoming a university teacher. He has published two volumes of poetry: *Concerto for an Exile* (Heinemann, 1973); *The Graveyard Also Has Teeth* (Heinemann, 1980).

Looking for the Spirit at Night

Before my house drinking the peaceful frangipanis
a family of coconut palms shading the nudity of the beach
before my house the termite-infected lemon trees
and the slow movement of the iguana on the iroko tree
it is here that I hear the concerto for death
the wailing cicadas and the howling bats
and the monotonous croaking of the frogs
Sierra Leone with its sad eyes and the medicinal impulse
of a late vulture clearing carcasses off the road
are they brothers of the soul or skeletons of the hour 10

tonight being Sunday Juba is humid and feeling this heat
I think I'll like to open the antennae of my head
to catch one word one flowering word of hope
before the rain which threatens the night
here where I await the spirit come to live with me
for to be a brother of that spirit . . . Manfred
I write you I call you I make this poem a fountain of your memory
where I drink your delicate fragrance
and then I can walk through open doors
searching for you hoping that your face is no more a shadow 20
that you are no more bronze than flesh
brother!

but tonight is so peaceful I am drinking my soul
the cicadas the iguana the vulture and the frogs
the termites the beach the gigantic moths
the invading butterflies chased by the geckos
and the matter-of-fact overdose of my deadly solitude!

JOHN PEPPER CLARK

Nigerian poet and playwright, born in 1935 in the Ijaw country of the Niger Delta. Studied at Ibadan University, where he founded the poetry magazine called *The Horn.* He worked as a journalist in Nigeria before becoming a university teacher. His poetry includes: *Poems* (Mbari, 1962); *A Reed in the Tide* (Longman, 1965); *Casualties: Poems 1966-68* (Longman, 1970); *A Decade of Tongues: Selected Poems 1958-68* (Longman, 1981).

You May Well Cry

(from *The Song of a Goat)*

You may well cry. But this is nothing
To beat your breast. It was how
We all began and will end. A child,
Once out of the womb, will shout,
Even like the chick or seedling
Out of its shell. And whether
For pain, for laugh, who can tell? But now you
Have lived to this day, perhaps you are ripe
To hazard a crack at life's nut. Still,
Do not, my people, venture overmuch 10
Else in unravelling the knot, you
Entangle yourselves. It is enough
You know now that each day we live
Hints at why we cried out at birth.

Night Rain

What time of night it is
I do not know
Except that like some fish
Doped out of the deep
I have bobbed up bellywise
From stream of sleep
And no cocks crow.

It is drumming hard here
And I suppose everywhere
Droning with insistent ardour upon 10
Our roof thatch and shed
And thro' sheaves slit open
To lightning and rafters
I cannot quite make out overhead
Great water drops are dribbling
Falling like orange or mango
Fruits showered forth in the wind
Or perhaps I should say so
Much like beads I could in prayer tell
Them on string as they break 20
In wooden bowls and earthenware
Mother is busy now deploying
About our roomlet and floor.
Although it is so dark
I know her practised step as
She moves her bins, bags and vats
Out of the run of water
That like ants filing out of the wood
Will scatter and gain possession
Of the floor. Do not tremble then 30
But turn, brothers, turn upon your side
Of the loosening mats
To where the others lie.
We have drunk tonight of a spell
Deeper than the owl's or bat's
That wet of wings may not fly.
Bedraggled up on the iroko, they stand
Emptied of hearts, and
Therefore will not stir, no, not
Even at dawn for then 40
They must scurry in to hide.
So let us roll over on our back
And again roll to the beat
Of drumming all over the land
And under its ample soothing hand
Joined to that of the sea
We will settle to a sleep of the innocent and free.

Ibadan

Ibadan,
        running splash of rust
and gold – flung and scattered
among seven hills like broken
china in the sun.

Incident at the Police Station, Warri

(after *The Flagellation of Jesus*
by Piero della Francesca)

Stripped to his penis, the convict at
His lordship's command is shooed out
Of his cell into the square to a bench,
Gleaming with grime in the sun.
'Lie down!' cracks the order, and at that,
Superfluous uniform hands as of an octopus
Grapple the prisoner down, one smart
Sergeant mounting his back. Now with the hiss
And beat of a cobra incensed,
The big stick descends deliberate and   10
Constant upon the shivering buttocks till
Carbolic water, blood, and tears, wrung
Free in spite of iron will,
Flow in one polluted stream, washing
Society of another individual wrong.
And the smell
Fills the air of the first flagellation with thong:
The scared, curious throng,
Mainly of women and children, twittering
At the sight of a tail shrunken   20
Between thighs, three very important
Looking persons discussing in one corner,
Perhaps the latest list of promotions or
Prices on the market, and in a car
Parked close by, one gallant and another
Asking the girls to more wine and song.

The Casualties

The casualties are not only those who are dead;
They are well out of it.
The casualties are not only those who are wounded,
Though they await burial by instalment.
The casualties are not only those who have lost
Persons or property, hard as it is
To grope for a touch that some
May not know is not there.
The casualties are not only those led away by night;
The cell is a cruel place, sometimes a haven, 10
Nowhere as absolute as the grave.
The casualties are not only those who started
A fire and now cannot put it out. Thousands
Are burning that had no say in the matter.
The casualties are not only those who escaping
The shattered shell become prisoners in
A fortress of falling walls.
The casualties are many, and a good number well
Outside the scenes of ravage and wreck;
They are the emissaries of rift, 20
So smug in smoke-rooms they haunt abroad,
They do not see the funeral piles
At home eating up the forests.
They are the wandering minstrels who, beating on
The drums of the human heart, draw the world
Into a dance with rites it does not know

The drums overwhelm the guns. . .
Caught in the clash of counter claims and charges
When not in the niche others have left,
We fall, 30
All casualties of the war,
Because we cannot hear each other speak,
Because eyes have ceased to see the face from the crowd,
Because whether we know or
Do not know the extent of wrong on all sides,
We are characters now other than before

The war began, the stay-at-home unsettled
By taxes and rumours, the looters for office
And wares, fearful every day the owners may return,
We are all casualties, 40
All sagging as are
The cases celebrated for kwashiorkor,
The unforeseen camp-follower of not just our war.

The Lagos-Ibadan Road before Shagamu

A bus groaned uphill. Trapped
In their seats, fifty odd passengers rocked
To its pulse, each dreaming
Of a different destination.
GOD'S TIME IS THE BEST, read
One legend. NO CONDITION IS
PERMANENT, said another. And on,
On over the hill Ashiru
Drove the lot, a cloud of Indian hemp
Unfolding among his robes. With 10
The swish over his shoulders, it
Trailed out, touched tails with the smoke
That squatted all indigo
On the hillside: like a stream
Was the going downhill, swift
Past recollection, straight into a bend
Upturned as a saucer, and
The journey spilt over in a ditch.
In the early morning sun,
To the clamour of flies that first 20
Answered the alarm, water
Of sewage kind washed their common
Wound, silenced their common groan.
No need of first aid,
All died on the spot,
Said the dailies. *The police,*
Well supplied with notes,
Are looking for the driver
Who escaped unhurt.

BERNARD B. DADIE

Born in 1916 near Abidjan, Ivory Coast. He was educated in Dakar and for some years worked there for the Institut Français d'Afrique Noire, before returning to the Ivory Coast to enter government service. He has published a number of prose works and plays, as well as three volumes of poetry: *Afrique debout* (Seghers, 1950); *La Ronde des jours* (Seghers, 1956); *Hommes de tous les continents* (Présence Africaine, 1967).

The Lines of Our Hands

The lines of our hands
Are not parallel lines
Nor roads through the mountains
Nor fissures on tree trunks
Nor the scars of Homeric fights.

The lines of our hands
Are not longitude lines

Nor furrows in the plains
Nor partings in the hair
Nor paths through the bush 10

No they are not
  gutters for grief
  channels for tears
  drainage for hate
  ropes for the hanged
  nor portions
  nor parts
  nor pieces
    of this . . . and that . . .

The lines of our hands 20
  not Yellow
  Black
  White

No they are not frontiers
Ditches between our villages
Cords to bind faggots of bitterness

The lines of our hands
Are the lines of Life,
    of Fate,
    of Heart, 30
    of Love.

Gentle bonds
To bind us
To one another
The living to the dead.

The lines of our hands
    not white
    not black
    not yellow

The lines of our hands 40
Bind the nosegays of our dreams.

Translated from the French

Leaf in the Wind

I am the man the colour of Night
Leaf in the wind, I go at the drift of my dreams.

I am the tree putting forth shoots in spring
The dew that hums in the baobab's hollow.

Leaf in the wind, I go at the drift of my dreams.

I am the man they complain of
Because opposed to formality
The man they laugh at
Because opposed to barriers.

Leaf in the wind, I go at the drift of my dreams. 10

I am the man they talk about:
  'Oh him!'
Him you cannot hold
The breeze that touches you and is gone

Leaf in the wind, I go at the drift of my dreams.

Captain at the stern
Scanning the scudding clouds
For the earth's powerful eye;
Ship without sail
That glides on the sea 20

Leaf in the wind, I go at the drift of my dreams.

I am the man whose dreams
Are manifold as the stars
More murmurous than swarms of bees
More smiling than children's smiles
More sonorous than echoes in the woods.

Leaf in the wind, I go at the drift of my dreams.

Translated from the French

JOE DE GRAFT

Born in 1924 in Ghana. Best known as a playwright, he published an epic play *Muntu* (Heinemann, 1977). He also published a volume of poetry, *Beneath the Jazz and Brass* (Heinemann, 1975) and a selection of his poems was published in the anthology, *Messages: Poems from Ghana* (Heinemann, 1971). He died in 1978.

The Rock behind the Fort

Under the eaves of the filling station
  A lunatic escaped from the asylum snores gently,

Double-bent in sleep like a broken lobster;
Two prostitutes drift homewards,
Misty with fatigue
Musky with many males;
A tattered watchman on his rounds,
His smoky lantern swaying,
Returns to his dew-sodden mattress
In the shadow of the warehouse: 10
Humanity lives on, thankfully free
Though demented and broken
Forsaken, exploited and sleepless;
And I walk on in this very early dawn.

As I come to the front of the old fort –
Once its steaming, smelly dungeons
The last habitation this side of the world
For slaves
(Those barbaric days of long ago!) –
Three black prison vans arrive 20
Sweating with dew from their night journey
From the heart of the country
To this – their unknown destination.
Slowly, smoothly,
Like a well-tended engine of torture
In its first unhurried stirrings,
The black gates of the fort swing open;
This cannot be our last farewell to them,
These men who sought life's justification
In their battling against injustice; 30
The cause of Freedom and of Justice is not lost;
The sea destroys
The sea unknowing also builds.
Salt of the sea, preserve them;
Spray from the sea, shower on them grace;
Rock ancient as time
Give them of your strength.

BIRAGO DIOP

Born in 1906 in Dakar, Senegal. A veterinary surgeon by profession, since the independence of Senegal he has been an ambassador and a government minister. He is best known for his collections of folk-tales, but he has also published a volume of poetry entitled *Leurres et Lueurs* (Presence Africaine, 1960).

Viaticum

In one of the three vessels
The three vessels where certain evenings come
The souls serene and satisfied,
The breathings of the ancestors,
Ancestors who once were men
Forefathers who once were sages
My mother dipped three fingers,
Three fingers of her left hand:
Thumb and index and second finger;
And I myself dipped three fingers; 10
Three fingers of the right hand:
Thumb and index and second finger.
With three fingers red in the blood,
Blood of dog,
Blood of bull,
Blood of goat,
My mother three times touched me.
She touched my forehead with her thumb,
With her index my left breast
And with her second finger touched my navel, 20
I myself held out my fingers red in the blood
Blood of dog,
Blood of bull
Blood of goat,
I held out my three fingers to the winds
To the winds from the North, to the winds from the East
To the winds from the South, to the winds from the Sunset;
And I raised my three fingers to the Moon,
To the full Moon, the Moon naked and full
At the bottom of the largest vessel. 30

When I had plunged my fingers into the sand
Into the sand which had grown cold
Then my Mother said: 'Go, go through the World
All your life they will follow your steps.'

And now I go
I go down the paths
Down the paths and the roads,
Beyond the sea and further, and further still
Beyond the sea and beyond what is beyond
And when I come near to the wicked, 40
To the men with black hearts
When I come near to the envious
To the men with black hearts
The Breathings of my Forefathers go before me.

Translated from the French

Breath

Listen more to things
Than to words that are said.
The water's voice sings
And the flame cries
And the wind that brings
The woods to sighs
Is the breathing of the dead.

Those who are dead have never gone away.
They are in the shadows darkening around,
They are in the shadows fading into day, 10
The dead are not under the ground.
They are in the trees that quiver,
They are in the woods that weep,
They are in the waters of the rivers,
They are in the waters that sleep.
They are in the crowds, they are in the homestead.
The dead are never dead.

Listen more to things
Than to words that are said.
The water's voice sings 20
And the flame cries
And the wind that brings
The woods to sighs
Is the breathing of the dead.
Who have not gone away
Who are not under the ground
Who are never dead.

Those who are dead have never gone away.
They are at the breast of the wife.
They are in the child's cry of dismay 30
And the firebrand bursting into life.
The dead are not under the ground.
They are in the fire that burns low
They are in the grass with tears to shed,
In the rock where whining winds blow
They are in the forest, they are in the homestead.
The dead are never dead.

Listen more to things
Than to words that are said.
The water's voice sings 40
And the flame cries
And the wind that brings
The woods to sighs
Is the breathing of the dead.

And repeats each day
The Covenant where it is said
That our fate is bound to the law,
And the fate of the dead who are not dead
To the spirits of breath who are stronger than they.
We are bound to Life by this harsh law 50
And by this Covenant we are bound
To the deeds of the breathings that die
Along the bed and the banks of the river,
To the deeds of the breaths that quiver
In the rock that whines and the grasses that cry

To the deeds of the breathings that lie
In the shadow that lightens and grows deep
In the tree that shudders, in the woods that weep,
In the waters that flow and the waters that sleep,
To the spirits of breath which are stronger than they 60
That have taken the breath of the deathless dead
Of the dead who have never gone away
Of the dead who are not now under the ground.

Listen more to things
Than to words that are said.
The water's voice sings
And the flame cries
And the wind that brings
The woods to sighs
Is the breathing of the dead. 70

Translated from the French

DAVID DIOP

Born in Bordeaux, France, in 1927, of a Senegalese father and a Cameroonian mother. Published a small volume of verse *Coups de pilon* (Présence Africaine, 1956), which showed great promise and has proved very popular. He was killed in an air crash in 1960. His poetry has been translated into English under the title *Hammer Blows* (Heinemann, 1975).

Waves

The wild breakers of freedom
Lash, lash the maddened Beast
From yesterday's slave springs a soldier
The Suez docker, the Hanoi coolie
All those poisoned with fatal creeds
Fling their huge song into the breakers
The wild breakers of freedom
Lashing, lashing the maddened Beast.

Translated from the French

Defiance against Force

You, bowing, you, crying
You, dying, like that, one day without knowing why.
You, struggling, you watching over another's rest
You, looking no longer with laughter in your eyes
You, my brother, your face full of fear and suffering
    Stand up and shout NO!

Translated from the French

Times

There are times for dreaming
In the calm of nights by the hollow of silence
There are times for doubting
And the heavy veil of words is torn with sighs
There are times for suffering
Along the roads of war under our mothers' eyes
There are times for loving
In the huts of light where the unique flesh sings
There is what colours the days to come
As the sun colours the flesh of plants   10
And in times of madness
In times of impatience
There is always the most fruitful seed
Of the times that bring the poised and certain stance.

Translated from the French

Africa

Africa my Africa
Africa of proud warriors in the ancestral savannahs
Africa my grandmother sings of
Beside her distant river
I have never seen you
But my gaze is full of your blood

Your black blood spilt over the fields
The blood of your sweat
The sweat of your toil
The toil of slavery 10
The slavery of your children
Africa, tell me Africa,
Are you the back that bends
Lies down under the weight of humbleness?
The trembling back striped red
That says yes to the sjambok on the roads of noon?
Solemnly a voice answers me
'Impetuous child, that young and sturdy tree
That tree that grows
There splendidly alone among white and faded flowers 20
Is Africa, your Africa. It puts forth new shoots
With patience and stubbornness puts forth new shoots
Slowly its fruits grow to have
The bitter taste of liberty.'

Translated from the French

MBELLA SONNE DIPOKO

Born in 1936 in Douala, Cameroon, but grew up in Western Cameroon and Nigeria. He worked for the Nigerian Broadcasting Corporation before going to Paris where he has lived since 1960. He has published two novels and a volume of poetry entitled *Black and White in Love* (Heinemann, 1972).

Autobiography

We crawled and cried and laughed
Without hope
Without despair.
We grew up
Fenced in by the forest.

But this world of uncles and fathers and mothers and others
Our fine world of greenness and grins was blown away
By the terrible storm of growth
And the mind soon flung pebbles at the cranes of the off-shore island.

But today 10
Floods flee the rising sun
And owls hoot from the edge of the dark song.
Like cripples blinded by sandy winds
Dreams drift under the low sky of our sleep
And our hearts listen to the voice of days in flight
Our thoughts dusting the past.

My Brother and I Left the Apartment

(from *The Return from Tangier*)

My brother and I left the apartment.
He went to live at a friend's
And I went to live by candle-light
In unused corridors
Sometimes spending the night in my sleeping bag in alleyways
Until in a round-up of layabouts
One morning the Parisian police picked me up.
We were driven to a prison outside Paris
And in the big police van
We bums called one another brothers and sisters 10
And there was the smell of red wine and of piss
And some of the sisters had bloated red faces.
And one of the brothers
A thin heavily-bearded man in his late forties maybe
Talked all the time to himself
With the haughty intensity of one
Who despises human affairs.

At the prison
The women were separated from the men
Just before we were led to the showers
Where at the order of the Republic

We had to wash away for a while
All the moondust and stardust
Of our free lives in the open
And we were made to dress in Chinese-style uniforms
And *sabots* for shoes.
There was well-starched and ironed excrement
In the pockets of my uniform
A former prisoner must have emptied his bowels into those pockets
Which the Police laundrymen hadn't cared to turn out
Because prisoners aren't allowed
Anything on their persons.

We were served breakfast
Then confined to collective cells
And some of the brothers were false brothers
Being clearly plain-clothes officers planted on us
To listen to whatever we said
But they paid no attention to the brother who talked to himself
For the abundance of his words was of a world
Where the laws of man do not apply
And the soul is free to invoke night and day
In the same breath.

We were served a lunch of bread, potatoes and cattle guts,
After which we returned to the cells
And those of us who hadn't police records
Were released later in the day
And I felt wonderful carrying my sleeping bag
And copies of the left-wing newspaper
I had been selling the previous evening
And walking out of that place.
But if I should be picked up a second time
They'll put me in jail for vagrancy
Which might happen any day
Unless these poems attain on earth
The popularity I feel is theirs in the skies
Where the gods read by the light of the stars.

Most of the brothers and sisters have returned
To the Place de la Contrescarpe

And the rue de la Montagne Sainte Genevieve
And the other bum places
Where they sit in twos or threes
Drinking red wine and despising and abusing the world.
As I come by, my hair and beard shabby and overgrown
And carrying my bag of manuscripts and newspapers
We exchange greetings and they beg
And if it is a good day I do what I can.

MALICK FALL

Born in 1920 in Senegal. He has worked in the Senegalese Department of Information and as a diplomat. He has published a novel and a volume of poems entitled *Reliefs* (Présence Africaine, 1964).

Schoolboys

I went to school bare-footed my head crammed
Stories and legends all abuzz
Up to my ears in the sounding air
My books and my juju fought together
In my satchel and in my head

I rode to school on the tide of my dreams
In the age-old wake my totems draw
I settled the wrong way round in my seat
I sniggered at what the master said

You wear your eagerness to school 10
Receptive mind ready to bear
Humiliations with a cheerful heart

You go to school in Homer's company
With Eluard's poems and Perrault's tales

But remember Kotje as you pass his shrine.

Translated from the French

Empty Head

An idea came
Into my head
So slender
So slight
An idea came
Fleetingly
Fearfully
Came to alight
It wheeled about
Stretched itself out 10
An idea came
That I wanted to stay
But it brushed my hand
And taking its flight
Through my fingers
Slipped away.

Translated from the French

PASCAL MAFIKA GWALA

Born in 1946 in Verulam, South Africa. He has worked as a legal clerk, school teacher and factory worker. He edited *Black Review 1973* and has published one volume of verse, *Jol'iinkomo* (Ad. Donker, 1977).

One Small Boy Longs for Summer

The kettle hisses
Mother moves about the kitchen
sliding from corner to corner.
The fire from the stove
pierces into the marrow.
And mother pushing towards the stove
warns of the steam.
My young brother, Thamu, jerks my arm
violently: Stop leaning on me, your elbow

has sunk into my thigh. 10
            Apology
                  I wasn't aware.

The kettle sings
            Some distant far-away song?
Mother picks it up
with an almost tender care.
Sets me thinking of a war-picture
The actor carefully setting the charge
and smiling all the time
                  I'll also be a soldier 20
when I'm old – why, Uncle Shoba was one.
Father drops the paper on the table
He comes to join us
            – staring coldly round.
It's no frown really,
But he's grinding his jaws.
            Maybe it's the July
Handicap.

The kettle purrs now
Steam is escaping; it kisses the ceiling 30
and vanishes. Mother is pouring the violent waters
into the coffee-jug. Coffee.
Yes, I need some coffee – a mug of hot coffee.
Very rousing.
We can't play outside – I must not go, I know
            How we danced in the rain. We are so tired
of the winter: It's so dingy outside.
We can't play inside – I'm so tied up.
It's so boring, I feel like bursting into
a cracking laughter; but father, 40
he'll go mad.
It's so steamy inside
I feel I could bite the walls down.
If only it makes the winter pass.

MAZISI KUNENE

Born in 1930 in Durban, South Africa. Studied at Natal University and became head of the Department of African Studies in the University College of Roma, Lesotho. After leaving southern Africa, he became a founder member of the Anti-Apartheid Movement in Britain and has represented the African National Congress in Europe and the United States. He is now Associate Professor in African Literature and Languages at the University of California, Los Angeles. He is well known for his work on the Zulu epic and has published two epic poems entitled *Emperor Shaka the Great* (Heinemann, 1979) and *Anthem of the Decades* (Heinemann, 1981). In 1970 he published his first volume of verse, *Zulu Poems* (André Deutsch); his second volume, called *The Ancestors and the Sacred Mountain,* was published by Heinemann (African Writers Series) in 1982.

Place of Dreams

There is a place
Where the dream is dreaming us,
We who are the shepherds of the stars.
It stands towering as tall as the mountains
Spreading its fire over the sun
Until when we take one great stride
We speed with the eagle on our journey.
It is the eagle that plays its wings on our paths,
Wakening another blind dream.
Together with other generations hereafter 10
They shall dream them like us.
When they wake on their journeys they will say:
Someone, somewhere, is dreaming us, in the ruins.

The Gold-miners

Towers rise to the skies,
Sounds echo their music,
Bells ring backwards and forwards
Awakening the crowds from the centre of fire.

Attendants at the feast glitter,
Wealth piles on the mountains.
But where are the people?
We stand by watching the parades
Walking the deserted halls
We who are locked in the pits of gold. 10

A Heritage of Liberation

Since it was you who in all these thin seasons
Gave to our minds the visions of life,
Take these weapons for our children's children.
They were ours.
They broke the enemies' encirclements.
So let our children live with our voices
With all the plentifulness of our nightmares.
Let them bury us in the mountain
To remind them of our wanderings.
The sunset steals our youth 10
We must depart.
We must follow the trail of the killer-bird
Or else sleep the sleep of terror
To generations hereafter,
May they inherit our dream of the festival
We who watched the eagle roam over our heads
We who smelt the acrid smell of death
Who saw the vultures leave our comrade's flesh
We bequeath to you the rays of the morning . . .

Sword Eulogizing Itself after a Massacre

By the skills of broken men I was moulded
I reared my head proud of my heritage of steel
I tore into the bowels of men
And tasted the sweetness of blood.

My appetites were roused
Again and again I returned to the feast.
To hear the tales of foolish men;
They who boasted their feats of killing.
I lay down and watched their frightened eyes.

I was praised, 10
I the devourer of a thousand villages;
With reverence they carried me
To boast before the assemblies of men.

Satisfied
They sat down with me
Picking from me the particles of dust
And turning my face to all parts of the earth.
By the terror in their eyes I knew
The shadows of the dead haunted them
Tearing their minds to the voices of the innocent. 20

The Fearful Ruins

On the broken walls,
Bats hang away from the sun
Shadows of an ancient stranger
Cast their presence over our shoulders.
A pathway leads to the abandoned gate.
There frightened rats flee in terror.
The lone bird perches on the once favourite stone
She sings and blows away the afternoon
Everything falls suddenly into a fearful night.
Voices come back again and hang on a dry pole 10
They walk aimlessly
They speak to each other as though from memory.
But the winds carry them away
And cover their footsteps with desert dust.

The Great Ones

And the great ones are here
They have sat before the fire
Their hands glow in the deep flame
And their faces are sculptured in smoke
Their eyes wander slowly on the house-beams
Their voices begin to rise
Like humming bees in the middle of summer.
Their memories enter the body of the mountain
And they are possessed by the ancient poets
They sing for us their poem 10
They narrate the story of our beginnings.

In Praise of the Ancestors

Even now the Forefathers still live
They are not overcome by the power of the whirlwind.
The day that sealed their eyes did not conquer them.
Even the tall boulder that stands over them
Casts only a humble shadow over their resting place.
They are the great voice that carries the epics.
The Ancestors have come to listen to our songs,
Overjoyed they shake their heads in ecstasy.
With us they celebrate their eternal life.
They climb the mountain with their children 10
To put the symbol of the ancient stone on its forehead.
We honour those who gave birth to us,
With them we watch the spectacle of the moving mists.
They have opened their sacred book to sing with us.
They are the mystery that envelops our dream.
They are the power that shall unite us.
They are the strange truth of the earth.
They came from the womb of the universe.
Restless they are, like a path of dreams,
Like a forest sheltering the neighbouring race of animals. 20
Yes, the deep eye of the universe is in our chest.
With it we stare at the centres of the sky.
We sing the anthems that celebrate their great eras.
For indeed life does not begin with us.

BERNARD KOJO LAING

Born in 1946 in Kumasi, Ghana. Studied at Glasgow University. He has been an administrator in various districts of Ghana and in Accra, and is now Administrative Secretary at the Institute of African Studies, University of Ghana, Legon. His poems have been published in various journals in Ghana and Britain.

Jazz Song

Kokrokooooooooooh! I am the clean beach of Africa,
strong with the dance of coconut trees!
I crash onto the sand and force-wet the frightened shells!
Who will stop me except death.
I am the revelation of canoes with big engines!
I ride the great waves
like the easiest girl-horses of the world,
and when I sit down Storms come and pay homage to me!
I live right on through wrecks of sorrow,
I destroy old sea rites and create brand-new ones, 10
I slice the sea into two and swagger among the sharks!
Which one will dare bite me.
The bright-blue sky is my sole umbrella-beautiful,
The long roar of the waves is the cry of my long lions
hungry for that profound silence that only I contain.
Sing more to me with your voices of verve,
you ghosts of the deep!
Fishermen are my messengers, fish are my food,
rocks are my footrests, coconuts are my height of glory!
Where can I not go in the sea. 20
Kokrokooooooooooh!
To the sea and to courage!
To the rhythm and to the long dance!
To modern boats and sophisticated shells!
The song growls and darkens into storms,
The song bursts my flood-rain messages
over the greatest cities of Africa!
Kokrokooooooooooh! Yes! I am the clean beach of
the strongest coconut trees of the sun!

Bring It Here

Bring
your pain here,
                for
whenever I get it
I intend
to sell it
                on the stock exchange
                for no less than six pounds
                a terrible share.

Miles: Poem on a Runway

My heart is a crash for You!
   My ginger-ale love! My
one-way street of desires is closed, My
   memories are higher than aeroplanes.
These ripe pawpaws outside are messages, and
I chase flies away from clean fruit clean thoughts.
                              Your wild waist
                              Is a dangerous corner
      for my hand of overspeeding fingers:
gentleman crashes on his way to big embrace!   10
and there is wailing by the absent kiss!
      Quick I want the hug I never gave you,
   for your fine mouth is nothing,
                                    just a jump
         of two steps where I shiver below your wrists,
and land far away

TABAN LO LIYONG

Born in 1938 in Northern Uganda. He studied in Uganda and then in the United States, where he attended the Writers' Workshop at the University of Iowa, obtaining his MA in Fine Arts in 1968. He returned to East Africa and now lectures at the University of Nairobi. He has made a particular study of Lwo literature and published his own translations of Lwo poetry in a volume entitled *Eating Chiefs* (Heinemann, 1970). In addition to books of short stories and criticism, he has published two volumes of poetry: *Frantz Fanon's Uneven Ribs: Poems, More and More* (Heinemann, 1971); *Another Nigger Dead* (Heinemann, 1972).

Song from the Congolese

When I was young mother told me to shut up
  or else the ten-eyed giant would hear me.
When I was young mother told me to finish my food
  or else daddy would spank me dead.
When I was young sister told me to steal
  or else I would not get my meal.
When I was young mother told me to bathe
  or else the *akula* would catch me at night.
When I was young I was told to be home at night
  or else *abiba* would eat my liver. 10
When I was young teachers told me to pray at night
  or else Satan would be by my side.

Now that I am old the giant comes and visits me:
  I can see his red ten eyes and bloody teeth;
Now that I am old I can feel the hand of father
  when with rage he beats me as if I was a foe;
Now that I am old I still remember sister
  when hunger comes and gnaws my entrails;
Now that I am old I know the Black Maria for sure
  as the truck to take me for cutting up; 20
Now that I am old I know the eagle overhead is for sure
  that bird which eats my life while I am alive;
Now that I am old I go to pray
  in order to get some quiet.

OSWALD MTSHALI

Born in 1940 in Vryheid, South Africa. He left South Africa in 1974 for the United States but has recently returned. His first volume of poems, *Sounds of a Cowhide Drum* (Oxford University Press, 1972), has enjoyed considerable popularity since it was first published in South Africa. His second volume, *Fireflames* (Shuter & Shooter, 1980), has been banned in South Africa.

A Newly-Born Calf

A newly-born calf
is like oven-baked bread
steaming under a cellophane cover.
The cow cuts
the shiny coat
as a child would
lick a toffee
with a tongue as pink as
the sole of a foot.
The calf sways on legs 10
filled with jelly and custard
instead of bone and marrow;
and it totters
to suck the teats
of its mother's udder.

Pigeons at the Oppenheimer Park

I wonder why these pigeons in the Oppenheimer Park
are never arrested and prosecuted for trespassing
on private property and charged with public indecency.

Every day I see these insolent birds perched
on 'Whites Only' benches, defying all authority.
Don't they know of the Separate Amenities Act?

A white policeman in full uniform, complete
with a holstered .38 special, passes by
without even raising a reprimanding finger
at offenders who are flouting the law. 10
They not only sit on the hallowed benches,
they also mess them up with birdshit.

Oh! Holy Ideology! look at those two at the crest
of the jumping impala, they are making love in full
view of madams, hobos, giggling office girls.
What is the world coming to?
Where's the sacred Immorality Act? *Sies*!

A Brazier in the Street

Around the smoke-billowing brazier
huddled four urchins, smoking
cigarette stubs and swopping stories
like seamen telling tales over a bottle of rum.
    The wintry air nipped their navels
    as a calf would suck the nipple.
    Smoke, blowing into bleary eyes,
    and waving flames fashioned
    their bodies into crouching silhouettes.
One yawned – 10
and rubbed his sleep-laden eyes
and mumbled as if in a dream
'I once ate a loaf of bread with nothing . . .'

Then a buxom woman, blanketed
against the blistering chill,
came out of the house
and carried the red-hot brazier inside
to cook her supper

And quicker than a rabid dog
leaps to swallow its tail, 20
the starless night gaped
and gulped down the foursome.

Sunset

The sun spun like
a tossed coin.
It whirled on the azure sky,
it clattered into the horizon,
it clicked in the slot,
and neon-lights popped
and blinked 'Time expired',
as on a parking meter.

The Face of Hunger

I counted ribs on his concertina chest
bones protruding as if chiselled
by a sculptor's hand of famine.

He looked with glazed pupils
seeing only a bun on some sky high shelf.

The skin was pale and taut
like a glove on a doctor's hand.

His tongue darted in and out
like a chameleon's
snatching a confetti of flies. 10

O! child,
your stomach is a den of lions
roaring day and night.

Amagoduka at Glencoe Station

We travelled a long journey
through the wattle forests of Vryheid,
crossed the low-levelled Blood River
whose water flowed languidly
as if dispirited for the
shattered glory of my ancestors.

We passed the coalfields of Dundee –
blackheads in the wrinkled face
of Northern Zululand –
until our train ultimately came 10
to a hissing stop at Glencoe.

Many people got off
leaving the enraged train
to snort and charge at the night
on its way to Durban.

The time was 8 p.m.

I picked up my suitcase,
sagging under the weight of a heavy overcoat
I shambled to the 'non-European Males' waiting room.

The room was crowded 20
the air hung, a pall of choking odour,
rotten meat, tobacco and sour beer.

Windows were shut tight
against the sharp bite of winter.

Amagoduka sat on bare floor
their faces sucking the warmth
of the coal fire crackling in the corner.

They chewed dried bread
scooped corned beef with rusty knives,
and drank *mqombothi* from the plastic can 30
which they passed from mouth to mouth.

They spoke animatedly
and laughed in thunderous peals.

A girl peeped through the door,
they shuddered at the sudden cold blast,
jumped up to fondle and leer at her
'*Hau! ngena Sisi!* – Oh! come in sister!'

She shied like a frightened filly
banged the door and bolted.

They broke into a tumultuous laughter. 40

One of them picked up a guitar
plucked it with broken finger nails
caressed its strings with a castor oil bottle –

it sighed like a jilted girl.
'You play down! Phansi! Play D' he whispered.

Another joined in with a concertina,
its sound fluttered in flowery notes
like a butterfly picking pollen from flower to flower.

The two began to sing,
their voices crying for the mountains 50
and the hills of Msinga, stripped naked of
their green garment.

They crossed rivers and streams,
gouged dry by the sun rays,
where lowing cattle genuflected
for a blade of grass and a drop of water
on riverbeds littered with carcasses and bones.

They spoke of hollow-cheeked maidens
heaving drums of brackish water
from a far away fountain. 60

They told of big-bellied babies
sucking festering fingers
instead of their mothers' shrivelled breasts.

Two cockroaches
as big as my overcoat buttons
jived across the floor
snatched meat and bread crumbs
and scurried back to their hideout.

The whole group joined in unison:
curious eyes peered through frosted windows 70
'*Ekhaya bafowethu!* – Home brothers!'

We come from across the Tugela river,
we are going to EGoli! EGoli! EGoli!
where they'll turn us into moles
that eat the gold dust
and spit out blood.

We'll live in compounds
where young men are pampered
into partners for older men.

We'll visit shebeens 80
where a whore waits for a fee
to leave your balls burning
with syphilitic fire.

If the gods are with us –
Oh! beloved black gods of our forefathers
What have we done to you
Why have you foresaken us –
we'll return home
to find our wives nursing babies –
unknown to us 90
but only to their mothers and loafers.

AGOSTINHO NETO

Born in Angola in 1922. Studied medicine in Portugal, where he was imprisoned for political activities. He returned to Angola in 1959. He became leader of the M.P.L.A. and the first President of independent Angola (1975). He died in 1979. Most of Neto's poems have been published in the volume entitled *Sagrada esperança* (Livraria Sá da Costa Editora, Lisbon, 1974). There is an English translation, *Sacred Hope,* by M. Holness (Tanzania Publishing House, 1974).

Between

This distress at being human
when in the mudhole reptiles entrench
and worms make ready to consume a handsome child
in an obscene orgy of cruelty

This delight at being human
when the dawn comes up, sweet and strong
over the resounding intoxication of the hymn of earth
dismaying worms and reptiles

And between the distress and the delight
a great track from the Niger to the Cape 10
where marimbas and hands drums and hands voices and hands
raise in harmony the inaugural hymn of Africa to come.

Translated from the Portuguese

Night

I live
in the dark townships of the world
without light or life.

I go down the streets
feeling my way

propped on my shapeless dreams
stumbling in slavery
in my longing to be.

Townships for slaves
worlds of misery 10
dark townships

Where their wills are diluted
and men take one another
for things.

I go tumbling
down the unlit
unfamiliar streets
blocked with mystery and dread
on the arm of ghosts.

And the night is dark. 20

Translated from the Portuguese

Don't Ask Me for Smiles

Don't ask me for glory
while I still breathe
the cries
of those wounded in battle

Don't ask me for glory
I am the Unknown Soldier
of mankind

To the generals belong honours

My glory
is all I suffer 10
and have gone through

my smiles
all I have wept

Nor smiles nor glory

Only the stern face
of the man building the road
that must be travelled –
stone by stone
in difficult country

A face sad 20
from so much effort spent
– the effort of the unflagging who tire
at evening
after work is done

Unlaurelled head
I am not to be found
in the catalogue of human glory

I have not shown myself in life
and untamed woods
hide the paths 30
I must travel

But I shall find them
and follow them
whatever the price

Then
in the new catalogue
I shall show you my face
palm branches will crown it

I shall have for you
the smiles you ask. 40

Translated from the Portuguese

Kinaxixi

I liked to go and sit
on a bench in Kinaxixi
about six o'clock on a very hot evening
and just sit . . .

Someone else might come along
perhaps and sit
sit down beside me

Watching the black faces of the people
on their way up the road
unhurried 10
a world of want expressed in the mixed Kimbundo
of their talk

Watching the weary steps
of servants whose fathers were servants
seeking love here pride there
on the far side of whatever alcohol

Never happiness never hatred

After the sun went down
the lamps were lit
and I 20
might wander aimlessly on
thinking our life is simple after all
a bit too simple
if you are tired and have to go on walking

Translated from the Portuguese

ARTHUR NORTJE

Born in Outshoorn, South Africa, in 1942. He studied in South Africa before going to Jesus College, Oxford. After a period teaching in Canada, he returned to Oxford to work for a doctorate. He died in 1970 of an overdose of barbiturates. Two collections of his poems have been published posthumously: *Lonely against the Light* (Rhodes University, 1973); *Dead Roots* (Heinemann, 1973). A good selection of Nortje's poems was included in *Seven South African Poets,* edited by Cosmo Pieterse (Heinemann), published in 1971.

Song for a Passport.

The nimble razor smoothed the skin
gorging itself on lather scum.
The soap's round shoulders mollified
muscles that raged in the amorous night:
and in the new September tide
I gravitate to what is comely,
having tasted contumely
because my crust is black and hard.

In the mirror in the morning in a mood
melange such as one's swelling dream induces 10
I brief myself as you would were you near,
to whom my flesh was rainbow, heart was harsh.
Parting of ways exposed
love's tattered fabric
but the world rose
larger through the tears in bright enticement.

Who loves me so much not to let me go,
not to let me leave a land of problems?
O poet answer everything
so that the dull green voucher 20
can hold a shiny photograph
and miracles of destinations,
gold lettering endorsing many travels.

This world is grim and green, the houses
lie wrapped in mist from third-floor windows.
Glossy pages in the waiting-room feel
firm as leather and the print slides past.
Now interviews and checks are in the offing:
O ask me all but do not ask allegiance!

Letter from Pretoria Central Prison

The bell wakes me at 6 in the pale spring dawn
with the familiar rumble of the guts negotiating
murky corridors that smell of bodies. My eyes
find salutary the insurgent light of distances.
Waterdrops rain crystal cold, my wet face in
ascent from an iron basin
greets its rifled shadow in the doorway.

They walk us to the workshop. I am eminent,
the blacksmith of the block; these active hours
fly like sparks in the furnace, I hammer metals 10
with zest letting the sweating muscles
forge a forgetfulness of worlds more magnetic.
The heart being at rest, life peaceable,
your words filter softly through my fibres.

Taken care of, in no way am I unhappy,
being changed to neutral. You must decide
today, tomorrow, bear responsibility,
take gaps in pavement crowds, refine ideas.
Our food we get on time. Most evenings
I read books, Jane Austen 20
for elegance, agreeableness (Persuasion).

Trees are green beyond the wall, leaves through the mesh
are cool in sunshine
among the monastic white flowers of spring that floats
prematurely across the exercise yard, a square
of the cleanest stone I have ever walked on.

Sentinels smoke in their boxes, the wisps
curling lovely through the barbed wire.

Also music and cinema, yesterday double feature.
At 4 p.m. it's back to the cell, don't laugh 30
to hear how accustomed one becomes. You spoke
of hospital treatment – I see the smart nurses
bringing you grapefruit and tea – good
luck to the troublesome kidney.
Sorry there's no more space. But date your reply.

Native's Letter

Habitable planets are unknown or too
far away from us to be
of consequence. To be of
value to his homeland must the wanderer
not weep by northern waters, but love
his own bitter clay
roaming through the hard cities, tough
himself as coffin nails.

Harping on the nettles of his melancholy,
keening on the blue strings of the blood, 10
he will delve into mythologies perhaps
call up spirits through the night.

Or carry memories apocryphal
of Tshaka, Hendrik Witbooi, Adam Kok,
of the Xhosa nation's dream
as he moonlights in another country:

but he shall also have
cycles of history
outnumbering the guns of supremacy.

Now and wherever he arrives 20
extending feelers into foreign scenes

exploring times and lives,
equally may he stand and laugh,
explode with a paper bag of poems,
burst upon a million televisions
with a face as in a Karsh photograph,
slave voluntarily in some siberia
to earn the salt of victory.

Darksome, whoever dies
in the malaise of my dear land 30
remember me at swim,
and moving waters spilling through my eyes:
and let no amnesia
attack at fire hour;
for some of us must storm the castles
some define the happening.

Untitled

That that is lost and found again
seldom is as beautiful. Some lustre
rubbed off in the night amid the neon
usage. Some sound deadened in a dark chair.

You are saddened looking in a pawnshop:
in a dusty window, faded, and stained
see knick-knacks, gilt lamps, second-hand stock.
Some come to buy, some reluctantly refrain.

Few come to redeem from the miscellany. These
items may be wanted but the wherewithal 10
is lacking. You sit and read obituaries,
visit a barbershop, walk around in a fruitstall.

All Hungers Pass Away

All hungers pass away,
we lose track of their dates;
desires arise like births,
reign for a time like potentates.

I lie and listen to the rain
hours before full dawn brings
forward a further day and winter sun
here in a land where rhythm fails.

Wanly I shake off sleep,
stare in the mirror with dream-puffed eyes: 10
I drag my shrunken corpulence
among the tables of rich libraries.

Fat hardened in the mouth,
famous viands tasted like ash:
the mornings-after of a sweet escape
ended over bangers and mash.

I gave those pleasures up,
the sherry circuit, arms of a bland girl
Drakensberg lies swathed in gloom,
starvation stalks the farms of the Transvaal. 20

What consolation comes
drops away in bitterness.
Blithe footfalls pass my door
as I recover from the wasted years.

The rain abates. Face-down
I lie, thin arms folded, half-aware
of skin that tightens over pelvis.
Pathetic, this, the dark posture.

GABRIEL OKARA

Born in 1921 in the Ijaw district of the Niger Delta, Nigeria. He studied journalism in the United States and worked subsequently as Information Officer in Eastern Nigeria. He joined the Biafra cause in the Nigerian civil war. His important experimental novel, *The Voice,* was published in 1964, but his poetry was not collected and published in volume form until 1978 (*The Fisherman's Invocation,* Heinemann).

Were I to Choose

When Adam broke the stone
and red streams raged down to
gather in the womb,
an angel calmed the storm;

And I, the breath mewed
in Cain, unblinking gaze
at the world without
from the brink of an age

That draws from the groping lips
a breast-muted cry 10
to thread the years.
(O were I to choose)

And now the close of one
and thirty turns, the world
of bones in Babel, and
the different tongues within
are flames the head
continually burning.

And O of this dark halo
were the third head free. 20

And when the harmattan
of days has parched the throat
and skin, and sucked the fever
of the head away,

Then the massive dark
descends, and flesh and bone
are razed. And (O were I
to choose) I'd cheat the worms
and silence seek in stone.

You Laughed and Laughed and Laughed

In your ears my song
is motor car misfiring
stopping with a choking cough;
and you laughed and laughed and laughed.

In your eyes my ante-
natal walk was inhuman, passing
your 'omnivorous understanding'
and you laughed and laughed and laughed.

You laughed at my song,
you laughed at my walk. 10

Then I danced my magic dance
to the rhythm of talking drums pleading, but you shut your
eyes and laughed and laughed and laughed.

And then I opened my mystic
inside wide like
the sky, instead you entered your
car and laughed and laughed and laughed.

You laughed at my dance,
you laughed at my inside.

You laughed and laughed and laughed. 20
But your laughter was ice-block
laughter and it froze your inside froze
your voice froze your ears
froze your eyes and froze your tongue.

And now it's my turn to laugh;
but my laughter is not
ice-block laughter. For I
know not cars, know not ice-blocks.

My laughter is the fire
of the eye of the sky, the fire 30
of the earth, the fire of the air,
the fire of the seas and the
rivers fishes animals trees
and it thawed your inside,
thawed your voice, thawed your
ears, thawed your eyes and
thawed your tongue.

So a meek wonder held
your shadow and you whispered:
'Why so?' 40
And I answered:
'Because my fathers and I
are owned by the living
warmth of the earth
through our naked feet.'

One Night at Victoria Beach

The wind comes rushing from the sea,
the waves curling like mambas strike
the sands and recoiling hiss in rage
washing the Aladuras' feet pressing hard
on the sand and with eyes fixed hard
on what only hearts can see, they shouting
pray, the Aladuras pray; and coming
from booths behind, compelling highlife
forces ears; and car lights startle pairs
arm in arm passing washer-words back 10
and forth like haggling sellers and buyers –

Still they pray, the Aladuras pray
with hands pressed against their hearts
and their white robes pressed against
their bodies by the wind; and drinking
palmwine and beer, the people boast
at bars at the beach. Still they pray.

They pray, the Aladuras pray
to what only hearts can see while dead
fishermen long dead with bones rolling 20
nibbled clean by nibbling fishes, follow
four dead cowries shining like stars
into deep sea where fishes sit in judgement;
and living fishermen in dark huts
sit round dim lights with Babalawo
throwing their souls in four cowries
on sand, trying to see tomorrow.

Still, they pray the Aladuras pray
to what only hearts can see behind
the curling waves and the sea, the stars 30
and the subduing unanimity of the sky
and their white bones beneath the sand.

And standing dead on dead sands,
I felt my knees touch living sands –
but the rushing wind killed the budding words.

CHRISTOPHER OKIGBO

Born in 1932 near Onitsha, Eastern Nigeria. Studied Classics at Ibadan University. He was a librarian at the University of Nigeria at Nsukka and then West African manager for Cambridge University Press. He joined the Biafra cause during the Nigerian civil war and was killed in action near Nsukka in 1967. His poetry was initially published by Mbari in Nigeria – *Heavensgate* (1962); *Limits* (1964). A collected and revised edition, with new poems, was published posthumously in 1971 under the title *Labyrinths with Path of Thunder* (Heinemann).

For Georgette

In the chill breath of the day's waking,
comes the newcomer,

when the draper of May
has sold out fine green garments,

and the hillsides have made up their faces,
and the gardens, on their faces a painted smile:

such synthetic welcome at the cock's third siren;
when from behind the bulrushes 10

waking, in the teeth of the chill May morn,
comes the newcomer.

Come Thunder

Now that the triumphant march has entered the last street corners,
Remember, O dancers, the thunder among the clouds . . .

Now that laughter, broken in two, hangs tremulous between the teeth,
Remember, O dancers, the lightning beyond the earth . . .

The smell of blood already floats in the lavender-mist of the afternoon.
The death sentence lies in ambush along the corridors of power;
And a great fearful thing already tugs at the cables of the open air,
A nebula immense and immeasurable, a night of deep waters –
An irón dream unnamed and unprintable, a path of stone.

The drowsy heads of the pods in barren farmlands witness it, 10
The homesteads abandoned in this century's brush fire witness it:
The myriad eyes of deserted corn cobs in burning barns witness it:
Magic birds with the miracle of lightning flash on their feathers. . .

The arrows of God tremble at the gates of light,
The drums of curfew pander to a dance of death;

And the secret thing in its heaving
Threatens with iron mask
The last lighted torch of the century. . .

Hurrah for Thunder

Whatever happened to the elephant –
Hurrah for thunder –

The elephant, tetrarch of the jungle:
With a wave of the hand
He could pull four trees to the ground;
His four mortar legs pounded the earth:
Wherever they treaded,
The grass was forbidden to be there.

Alas! the elephant has fallen –
Hurrah for thunder – 10

But already the hunters are talking about pumpkins:
If they share the meat let them remember thunder.

The eye that looks down will surely see the nose;
The finger that fits should be used to pick the nose.

Today – for tomorrow, today becomes yesterday:
How many million promises can ever fill a basket . . .

If I don't learn to shut my mouth I'll soon go to hell,
I, Okigbo, town-crier, together with my iron bell.

Elegy for Alto

(with drum accompaniment)

And the horn may now paw the air howling goodbye. . .

For the Eagles are now in sight:
Shadows in the horizon –

The robbers are here in black sudden steps of showers, of caterpillars –
The eagles have come again,
The eagles rain down on us –

Politicians are back in giant hidden steps of howitzers, of detonators –
The Eagles descend on us,
Bayonets and cannons –

The robbers descend on us to strip us of our laughter, of our thunder – 10
The Eagles have chosen their game,
Taken our concubines –

Politicians are here in this iron dance of mortars, of generators –
The eagles are suddenly there,
New stars of iron dawn;

So let the horn paw the air howling goodbye. . .

O mother mother Earth, unbind me; let this be
        my last testament; let this be
The ram's hidden wish to the sword the sword's
        secret prayer to the scabbard – 20

The robbers are back in black hidden steps of detonators –

For beyond the blare of sirened afternoons, beyond
        the motorcades;
Beyond the voices and days, the echoing highways; beyond the latescence
Of our dissonant airs; through our curtained eyeballs,
        through our shuttered sleep,

Onto our forgotten selves, onto our broken images;
    beyond the barricades
Commandments and edicts, beyond the iron tables,
    beyond the elephant's 30
Legendary patience, beyond his inviolable bronze
    bust; beyond our crumbling towers –

Beyond the iron path careering along the same beaten track –

The glimpse of a dream lies smouldering in a cave,
    together with the mortally wounded birds.
Earth, unbind me; let me be the prodigal; let this be
    the ram's ultimate prayer to the tether. . .

An old star departs, leaves us here on the shore
Gazing heavenward for a new star approaching;
The new star appears, foreshadows its going 40
Before a going and coming that goes on forever. . .

OKOT P 'BITEK

Born in 1931 at Gulu, Northern Uganda. His university studies took him to Britain, and on returning to East Africa he taught at Makerere University in Uganda and in Kenya. He wrote prose and poetry in the Acoli language and gained a considerable reputation for his long poem *The Song of Lawino* (East African Publishing House [EAPH], 1966). He also published *Song of Ocol* (EAPH, 1970); *The Song of the Prisoner* (EAPH, 1970); *Two songs* (*The Song of the Prisoner,* and *The Song of Malaya*) (EAPH, 1971). He died in 1982.

The Song of Lawino
1. I Am Not Unfair to My Husband

I am not unfair to my husband,
I do not complain
Because he wants another woman
Whether she is young or aged!

Who has ever prevented men
From wanting women?

Who has discovered the medicine for thirst?
The medicines for hunger
And anger and enmity
Who has discovered them? 10
In the dry season the sun shines
And rain falls in the wet season.
Women hunt for men
And men want women!
When I have another woman
With whom I share my husband,
I am glad
A woman who is jealous
Of another, with whom she shares a man,
Is jealous because she is slow, 20
Lazy and shy,
Because she is cold, weak, clumsy!

The competition for a man's love
Is fought at the cooking place
When he returns from the field
Or from the hunt,

You win him with a hot bath
And sour porridge.
The wife who brings her meal first
Whose food is good to eat, 30
Whose dish is hot
Whose face is bright
And whose heart is clean
And whose eyes are dark
Like the shadows:
The wife who jokes freely
Who eats in the open
Not in the bed room,
One who is not dull
Like stale beer, 40
Such is the woman who becomes
The head-dress keeper.

I do not block my husband's path
From his new wife.
If he likes, let him build for her
An iron roofed house on the hill!
I do not complain,
My grass thatched house is enough for me.

I am not angry
With the woman with whom 50
I share my husband,
I do not fear to compete with her.

All I ask
Is that my husband should stop the insults,
My husband should refrain
From heaping abuses on my head.
He should stop being half-crazy,
And saying terrible things about my mother
Listen Ocol, my old friend,
The ways of your ancestors 60
Are good,
Their customs are solid
And not hollow
They are not thin, not easily breakable
They cannot be blown away
By the winds
Because their roots reach deep into the soil.

I do not understand
The ways of foreigners
But I do not despise their customs. 70
Why should you despise yours?

Listen, my husband,
You are the son of a Chief.
The pumpkin in the old homestead
Must not be uprooted!

2. Time Has Become

Time has become
My husband's master
It is my husband's husband.
My husband runs from place to place
Like a small boy,
He rushes without dignity.

And when visitors have arrived
My husband's face darkens,
He never asks you in,
And for greeting 10
He says
'What can I do for you?'

I do not know
How to keep the white man's time.
My mother taught me
The way of the Acoli
And nobody should
Shout at me
Because I know
The customs of our people! 20
When the baby cries
Let him suck milk
From the breast.
There is no fixed time
For breast feeding.

When the baby cries
It may be he is ill;
The first medicine for a child
Is the breast.
Give him milk 30
And he will stop crying,
And if he is ill
Let him suck the breast
While the medicine-man

Is being called
From the beer party.

Children in our homestead
Do not sleep at fixed times;
When sleep comes
Into their head 40
They sleep,
When sleep leaves their head
They wake up.

When a child is dirty
Give him a wash,
You do not first look at the sun!
When there is no water
In the house
You cannot wash the child
Even if it is time 50
For his bath!
Listen
My husband,
In the wisdom of the Acoli
Time is not stupidly split up
Into seconds and minutes,
It does not flow
Like beer in a pot
That is sucked
Until it is finished. 60

It does not resemble
A loaf of millet bread
Surrounded by hungry youths
From a hunt;
It does not get finished
Like vegetables in the dish.

A lazy youth is rebuked,
A lazy girl is slapped,
A lazy wife is beaten,

A lazy man is laughed at 70
Not because they waste time
But because they only destroy
And do not produce.

And when famine
Invades your villages
And women take their baskets
To go and beg food
In the next village
Strangers will sleep with them!
They will have your wives 80
And what can you say?

YAMBO OUOLOGUEM

Born in 1940 in Mali. He studied in France where he published his best-known work, the novel *Le Devoir de violence (Bound to Violence).* He has not published poetry in volume form.

Tomatoes

People think I'm a cannibal
But you know what people say

People see I've got red gums but who has
White ones
Up the tomatoes

People say there are not nearly so many tourists
Now
But you know
This isn't America and nobody
Has the money

People think it's my fault and are scared
But look

My teeth are white not red
I've not eaten anybody
People are rotten they say I scoff
Baked tourists
Or maybe grilled
Baked or grilled I asked
They didn't say anything just kept looking uneasily at my gums
Up the tomatoes

Everyone knows in an agricultural country there's agriculture
Up the vegetables

Everyone knows that vegetables
Well you can't live on the vegetables you grow
And that I'm quite well developed for someone underdeveloped
Miserable scum living off the tourists
Down with my teeth

People suddenly surrounded me
Tied me up
Threw me down
At the feet of justice

Cannibal or not cannibal
Answer

Ah you think you're so clever
So proud of yourself

Well we'll see I'm going to settle your account
Have you anything to say
Before you are sentenced to death

I shouted Up the tomatoes

People are rotten and women curious you know
There was one of these in the curious circle
In her rasping voice sort of bubbling like a saucepan
With a hole in it

Shrieked
Slit open his belly
I'm sure father is still inside

There weren't any knives
Naturally enough among the vegetarians
Of the western world
So they got a Gillette blade
And carefully
Slit
Slat
Plop
Slit open my belly

Inside flourishing rows of tomatoes
Watered by streams of palm wine
Up the tomatoes

Translated from the French

LENRIE PETERS

Born in 1932 in Banjul, Gambia (now Senegambia). He studied medicine in England, where he qualified as a surgeon in 1967. He worked in England before returning to Gambia. In addition to a novel, he has published three volumes of poetry; *Poems* (Mbari, 1964); *Satellites* (Heinemann, 1967); *Katchikali* (Heinemann, 1971). His *Selected Poetry* (Heinemann, 1981) includes a number of new poems.

Parachute

Parachute men say
The first jump
Takes the breath away
Feet in the air disturbs
Till you get used to it

Solid ground
Is now where you left it
As you plunge down
Perhaps head first
As you listen to 10
Your arteries talking
You learn to sustain hope

Suddenly you are only
Holding an open umbrella
In a windy place
As the warm earth
Reaches out to you
Reassures you
The vibrating interim is over

You try to land 20
Where green grass yields
And carry your pack
Across the fields

The violent arrival
Puts out the joint
Earth has nowhere to go
You are at the starting point

Jumping across worlds
In condensed time
After the awkward fall 30
We are always at the starting point.

You Talk to Me of 'Self'

You talk to me of 'self'
– the African self. The inner
workings of a man, his caste
the meaning of his life.

Senghor extols the beauty –
the African beauty. The
chocolate icing and mascara 'selves'
along the ports and river's edge

Go arrow-flight two hundred miles
and ask for 'self', but 10
when you find him, send
me word that I may see

Go into villages, not palaces;
look among goats and sheep
under pyramids of squalor
degradation, the moon's eclipse

Octogenarian breasts at twenty
enthroned in pools of urine
after child birth, whose future
is not theirs to mould or flirt with mirth 20

There is your 'Self' crushed
between the grinding wheel
of ignorance and the centuries;
the blood congealed in the baking sun

What Do You Do

What do you do
crouching together
silent, eyes fixed
like wild cats at dusk?

Only your arms move,
elbow length into the calabash
giving, sharing; mouths crunching,
room for one stranger more.

It is the day's blessing;
the evening meal binding together 10

for those who know hunger
eating is solemn time –

The day's benediction –
so turn no stranger from the door;
one seed, one grain of rice
must soothe the writhing entrails.

But what of the heart,
is that filled with sharing?
you look into the mirror of your grave
and end in darkness. 20

LEOPOLD SEDAR SENGHOR

Born in 1906 at Joal, Senegal. He was educated in Dakar and in Paris, where he studied at the Sorbonne. After the Second World War, he played a leading role in nationalist politics in French West Africa, becoming Preisident of Senegal in 1960; he retired in 1980. He was a co-founder, with Aimé Césaire, of the negritude movement, expounding its ideals throughout his career in his essays and books. He quickly established himself as the leading African poet writing in French, and has published a number of volumes of poetry: *Chants d'ombre* (Seuil, 1945); *Hosties noires* (Seuil, 1948); *Chants pour Naett* (Seghers, 1949); *Ethiopiques* (Seuil, 1956), *Nocturnes* (Seuil, 1961); *Lettres d'hivernage* (Seuil, 1973); *Poèmes* (collected edition) (Seuil, 1964 and 1974); *Elegies majeures* (Seuil, 1979). For English translations of some of the poems, see *L.S. Senghor: Prose and Poetry* edited by John Reed & Clive Wake (Heinemann, 1976).

All Day Long

All day long along the long straight rails
(Unbending will on the listless sands)
Across the dryness of Cayor and Baol where the arms of the baobabs
twist in anguish
All day long, all along the line

Through tiny stations, each exactly like the last, chattering little black girls uncaged from school
All day long, roughly shaken on the benches of the clanking, dust-covered wheezing, antique train
I come seeking to forget about Europe in the pastoral heart of Sine.

Translated from the French

Taga for Mbaye Dyob

(for a tama)

Mbaye Dyob! I will speak your name and your honour.
Dyob! I will hoist your name to the high mast of the ship returning, ring your name like the bell that sounds victory,
I will sing your name Dyobene! you who called me master and
Warmed me with your fervour in the winter evenings around the red stove that made us cold.
Dyob! You cannot trace back your ancestry and bring order into black history, your forefathers are not sung by the voice of the tama.
You who have never killed a rabbit, who went to ground under the bombs of the great vultures
Dyob! you who are not captain or airman or trooper, not even in the baggage train,
But a second-class private in the Fourth Regiment of the Senegal Rifles
Dyob, I will celebrate your white honour.

The girls of Gandyol will make you a triumphal arch with their curved arms, arms of silver and of red gold 10
Make you a path of glory with their precious cloths from the rivers of the South.
Then they will make you with their mouths a necklace of ivory, better to wear than a royal garment
Then they will cradle your steps, their voices will mingle with the waves of the sea
Then they will sing 'You have faced more than death, more than the tanks and the planes that defy all magic
'You have faced hunger, you have faced cold, and the humiliation of captivity.

'O bravely, you have been the footstool of griots and clowns
'You have put new nails in your cross so as not to desert your companions
'Not to break the unspoken pact
'Not to leave your load to your comrades, whose backs bend at each new start
'Whose arms grow weak each evening when there is one less hand to shake 10
'And the face grows darker lit by one less look, the eyes sunken, reflecting one less smile.'
Dyob! from Ngabu to the Walo, from Ngalam to the sea will rise the songs of the amber virgins
Let them be accompanied by strings of the kora, let them be accompanied by the waves and the winds
Dyob! I speak your name and your honour.

Translated from the French

Ndessé

Mother, they have written you are turning white, as the bush turns white at the end of the rains
When I should be your festival, gymnic feast for your harvests
Your fair season, with the unclouded seven times nine years, and the barns full to bursting with fine millet
Your champion *Kor-Sanou!* Like the palm-tree of Katamague
Head and swaying silver plume above all his rivals
And the women's hair fluttering at their shoulders and the hearts of the maidens in the tumult of their breasts.

I am here, Mother, before you, a soldier in shirt sleeves,
Dressed up in foreign words, where your eyes see only a set of sticks and tatters
If I could tell you, Mother! But you would hear an affected prattle, you would not understand
As when good Serer women make mock of the god, herdsmen of clouds 10
With a rattle of rifle shots over the jingle of *paragnesse* words.
Speak to me Mother. My tongue slips on our sonorous hard words.
You can make them gentle and soft, as you made them once for the son you loved.

The pious burden of my lie is heavy upon me
I am no longer an official with authority, a marabout with delighted disciples,
Europe has broken me like a wretched soldier under the pachydermatous paws of tanks
My heart is more bruised than my body was once, home from adventures far off on the magical shores of the Spirits.

I should have been, Mother, the flourishing palm-tree of your age, I would give you back the ecstasy of your young years.
Now I am only your little boy in pain, tossing and turning on his aching sides.
Now, I am only a little boy who remembers his mother's breast and cries.
Take me into the night that is lit by the confidence you are close
Tell me over again the old stories of black evenings so that I lose myself down roads without memory
Mother, I am a humbled soldier, fed with coarse millet.

Tell me the pride of my fathers.

Translated from the French

To the American Negro Soldiers

I did not recognize you in your prison of sad-coloured uniforms
I did not recognize you under that calabash helmet with no plume
I did not recognize the quavering whinny of your iron horses that drink but do not eat.
No longer the nobility of elephants but the barbaric clumsiness of monsters from the foretime of the world.
Under your closed faces I did not recognize you.
I only touched the warmth of your brown hand. I said my name, 'Afrika!'
And found again lost laughter, I greeted the ancient voice and the roar of the cascades of the Congo.
Brothers, I do not know if it was you who bombed the cathedrals, the pride of Europe
If you are the lightning that in God's hand burnt Sodom and Gomorrah.
No, you are the messengers of his mercy, breath of Spring after Winter. 10
For those who had forgotten laughter (using only an oblique smile)

Who had forgotten the salt taste of tears and the irritant smell of blood
You bring the springtime of Peace, hope at the end of waiting
And their night fills with a sweetness of milk, the blue fields of the sky
covered with flowers, softly the silence sings.
You bring the sun. The air throbs with liquid murmurs and crystalline
whistling and the silky beat of wings
Aerial cities are warm with nests.
Down streets running with joy, boys play with their dreams
Men dance before their machines, and catch themselves singing.
The eyelids of schoolgirls are rose petals, fruits ripen at the breasts of
virgins
The hips of the women . . . o sweetness . . . grow full and heavy. 20
Black brothers, warriors whose mouths are singing flowers . . .
O delight to live after Winter . . .
I greet you as the messengers of peace.

Translated from the French

Message

They sent me a swift courier
He crossed the violence of rivers, in the low rice-fields he waded up to
the navel.
It meant that their message was urgent.
I left my meal still steaming and my attention to many lawsuits.
Just a cloth. I took nothing against the dewy mornings.
Provisions for the journey, white words of peace to open the way for me
everywhere.
I too crossed the rivers, and the virgin ambushes of the forests,
Where lianas hung down, more treacherous than serpents.
I passed through the tribes that let fly a poisonous greeting.
But I did not lose the sign of my recognition 10
And the spirits watched over the breath of my nostrils.
I recognized the ashes of former camps, I recognized the hereditary
hosts.
We exchanged long speeches under the kailcedrats
We exchanged the ritual gifts.
And I came to Elissa, nest of falcons defying the Invader's pride.
I saw once more the ancient dwelling on the hillside, a village with its
long lowered eyelashes
To the Guardians of the Blood I recited the long message.

Murrain. Ruin of trade. Game laws. Middle-class respectability
The dry contempt that swells the bellies of captives.
The Prince answered. This is the exact imprint of his words 20
'Children how short your memories are. What did the koras sing to you?
'You decline the rose, I hear, and your ancestors are the Gauls.
'You are doctors of the Sorbonne, pot-bellied with degrees
'You amass scraps of paper – not even golden louis to count under the lamp like your father with his griping fingers
'Your daughters I hear paint their faces like prostitutes
'Through their promiscuous loves, our race grows paler.
'Are you any happier? Some trumpet goes wa wa wa
'And down there in the evenings you weep great fires and blood.
'Must the ancient drama, the epic be unfolded to you,
'Go to M'Bissel to Fa'oy. Recite the rosary of the sanctuaries which mark out the Great Way 30
'Take again the Royal Route. Meditate this Way of the Cross and of Glory.
'Your high priests will answer you. Voice of Blood.
'More lovely than the palm-trees are the Dead of Elissa, few were the wants of their bellies
'Their shield of honour never left them nor their loyal lance.
'They did not hoard up rags, or even guineas to adorn their dolls.
'Their flocks covered and hid their lands, such were their dwellings in the divine shadow of the fig-trees.
'And their barns were packed to bursting with the harvest of children.
'Voice of Blood! Things to be thought on!
'The conquerors will greet your step. Your children will be the white cross of your head.'
I heard the words of the Prince. 40
Herald of the Good News, such was his ivory message.

Translated from the French

Your Letter on the Sheet

Your letter on the sheet, beneath the sweet-smelling lamp,
Blue as a new shirt a young man smooths.
Humming to himself; as the sky and the sea and my dream
Your letter. And the sea has its salt, and the air milk, bread, rice,
  I say its salt
Life holds its sap and earth its meaning
The meaning of God and his movement.
Your letter life would not be life without
Your lips my salt my sun, my fresh air and my snow.

Translated from the French

And the Sun

And the sun, a ball of fire, down sloping to the dark red sea.
At the edge of the bush and the deep, I stray down the labyrinthine path.
It haunts me, that high proud scent, inflames my nostrils
Deliciously; haunts me and you, my double, haunt me.

The sun plunges into distress
Into a swarm of lights, into a tremor of furies, of colours and cries.
A canoe, fine as a needle in an immense sea, shows
An oarsman and his double.
The stones of Cap de Nase bleed when the lighthouse of the
  Mamelles shines
From afar. Sorrow like this prompts me to thought of you. 10

I think of you when I walk, when I swim,
Sitting, standing I think of you, morning and evening
At night when I weep, and yes, when I laugh
In speech, in self-communion and in silence
In my joys and my griefs. When I think and when I do not think
My dear I think of you.

Translated from the French

SIPHO SEPAMLA

Born in about 1932 near Krugersdorp, South Africa, but has lived all his life in Johannesburg. Trained as a teacher, he has not only taught but actively promoted theatre in South Africa. He edits the black reviews *New Classic* and *S'ketsh.* He has published a novel and three volumes of poetry: *Hurry Up To It* (Ad. Donker, 1975); *The Blues Is You In Me* (Ad. Donker, 1976); *The Soweto I Love* (Rex Collings, 1977).

The Loneliness Beyond

Like raindrops pattering
They come singly and in pairs
Then as a torrent the rush of feet
Shuffles onto platforms
Dragging the last strains of energy.

I've seen hearts palpitating
Behind a single maskless face
Tired from the hurrying of a city
Spirits maimed by commands.

I've heard the clicks of tongues 10
Laughter rising above the grouse of mouths
That never rest
From grinding complaints.

Like sheep herded into a kraal
They crowd numbered coaches
Hopeful of a safe landing.

I've watched the multitudes rub shoulders
And I've wondered what they do
With the loneliness beyond;

I've seen throngs of people 20
Disappear into little holes of resting
And I've pondered what might be happening
With the loneliness beyond.

A Ballad on the Thing

I walk I stop
I see the man come
I stop I walk
I see the man come

He looks and stares
I see the man come
He stares and looks
I see the man come

Run now I ask
I see the man come 10
Run now I ask
I see the man come

Where to I ask
I see the man come
Where to I ask
I see the man come

Look search I say
The Thing must be there
Look search I say
The Thing must be there 20

Don't panic you fool
I see the man come
Don't panic you fool
I see the man come

Oh, dash you coward
He's looking that way
Oh, dash you coward
He's looking that way

Now stop it you boy
He'll shoot and say thief 30

Now stop it you boy
He'll shoot and say thief

I pause to think
Digesting the moment
I pause to think
Digesting the moment

Dear gods and angels
Are you sure watching this
Dear gods and angels
Are you sure watching this 40

I see a brother
He's coming my way
I see a brother
He's coming my way

I step behind the brother
We are going one way
I step behind the brother
We are going one way

We pass the man smoking
Smoke lost in the air 50
We pass the man smoking
Smoke lost in the air

Thank God I sigh
He's now out of sight
Thank God I sigh
He's now out of sight

The Island

And so said the island

I am strong
no one nears me without a tremble
I have for many years dared the sea
to swallow me and my innards

I am strong
the whole world knows of me
men talk loudly of their wishes for me
but none can walk on my shores

I am strong 10
I've for long held great secrets in my heart
I've known men of royal blood as well
but it's been the common man I've always feared

I am strong
I've broken the backs of many men
I've even tampered with their sanity
but as many have left me defiant

I am strong
my grip will drain the blood of anyone
see how Mandela & Sisulu have grown grey 20
but their spirits still defy me

I am strong
I wear wrinkles of age on my face
yet my eyes have been known not to blink
but rumour has it I'll be deserted one day

I am strong
but my courage has begun to seep out

Words, Words, Words

We don't speak of tribal wars anymore
we say simply faction fights
there are no tribes around here
only nations
it makes sense you see
'cause from there
one moves to multinational
it makes sense you get me
'cause from there
one gets one's homeland 10
which is a reasonable idea
'cause from there
one can dabble with independence
which deserves warm applause
– the bloodless revolution

we are talking of words
words tossed around as if
denied location by the wind
we mean those words some spit
others grab 20
dress them up for the occasion
fling them on the lap of an audience
we are talking of those words
that stalk our lives like policemen
words no dictionary can embrace
words that change sooner than seasons
we mean words
that spell out our lives
words, words, words
for there's a kind of poetic licence 30
doing the rounds in these parts

In Search of Roots

We will have to use animal fat
and not bother with cosmetics and so on

we will have to spill blood
just so that we keep contact with our ancestors

we will have to read time from the sun
and stop hurting our wrists

we will have to drink home beer
and give up potent spirits and things

we will have to seek out
black, green and golden flowers 10

we will have to speak up
because for too long others have spoken for us

we will have to laugh hard
even if it is at our own illusions

we will need to do all these things
just to show the world Africa was never discovered

MONGANE WALLY SEROTE

Born in 1944 in Sophiatown, South Africa. In the early seventies he studied at Columbia University, New York, where he took a degree in Fine Arts. He now lives in Botswana. He has published four volumes of poetry: *Yakhal'inkomo* (Renoster Books, 1972); *Tsetlo* (Ad. Donker, 1974); *No Baby Must Weep* (Ad. Donker, 1975); *Behold Mama, Flowers* (Ad. Donker, 1978).

For Don M. – Banned

it is a dry white season
dark leaves don't last, their brief lives dry out
and with a broken heart they dive down gently headed for the earth,
not even bleeding.
it is a dry white season brother,
only the trees know the pain as they still stand erect
dry like steel, their branches dry like wire,
indeed, it is a dry white season
but seasons come to pass.

Ofay-Watcher, Throbs-Phase

Phase I

In my soul,
Where peace lies like the darkness of sleeping eyes,
The quietness is now and then struck;
Struck, struck by a heart-beat like memory
That, in the beginning,
In the beginning things started to walk with one foot,
The other foot having been chopped off by time.

Phase II

My heart did not beat but limped,
Tears that dropped and made noise
In the unlit quiet of childhood corridors 10
Where adult faces were as blank as unpainted walls.

Phase III

Some stranger passing by threw a seed;
The tree of home is brown and green
I have seen it dry out as though to be dust,
I have seen its leaves green and fresh like the body of a river
But the face of the sun is grim.

Phase IV

I come from there,
The children there have no toys, they play with mud,
The boys and girls have nothing to do,
Their minds are laboratories and their bodies apparatus; 20
I come from down there,
The parents there are children of other men and women,
There the old just sit and wait for death
Like people wait for a train.
I come from down there below,
My friends are tender people who look old,
They are wild,
Like rats living in an empty room,
They are meek like sheep following the other blindly.
They and I come from down there below, 30
Down there below the bottom.

Phase V

In this pit filled with many blinking eyes,
My heart has licked and tasted mercy;
At times death just lies there, and you lick it like cats their kittens
But haai, the radio, newspapers,
Which come there like lying fortune tellers:
When educated people talk,
It's like waiting in a queue
And the bus does not come:
It's heavy. 40
Why?
The sea is very old
It is like I'm sleeping with my eyes, seeing the peace of closed eyes,
It is like I'm sleeping with my ears listening
When I watch the sea.
Why?
I want to know
Why is it nice at times,
When people don't talk –
Why? 50
And people like to talk –
Why?

Phase VI

My mother and my father are like Christ.
Forgive them because they know what they did:
I came here.

Phase VII

My younger brother is quiet, like a tree holding its leaves,
Not to shake,
But the wind is blowing.

Phase VIII

My younger sister is a seed
Or has a seed. 60

Phase IX

I love to watch the sky,
It is blank.
Why?
When the quiet of rattling leaves comes to my ears,
It's like watching people through the restaurant window at Park Station.

Phase X

People are like flowers:
Far, they attract you.
Bring them into the house,
In a vase, flowers die.

Phase XI

I read somewhere, 70
I read a story
It was sad.
A child on its mother's back,
Tasted with it's back, tasted a bullet –
It died.
I saw somewhere
8th Avenue, there,
My eyes closed,

The car knocked the child,
The child was playing in the street. 80
It died.

Phase XII

God,
How do we say sorry,
So they can understand, that we mean sorry?
The bodies that were opened
Cut
And bled in the street
While your stars watched, your moon watched, your sky watched
And your darkness cloaked the killer to look just like us.
And when your sun lights 90
We can see the tears
Of mothers, wives, women.
God,
How do we say sorry,
So they understand, that we mean sorry?

Phase XIII

White people are white people,
They are burning the world.
Black people are black people,
They are the fuel.
White people are white people, 100
They must learn to listen.
Black people are black people,
They must learn to talk.

Phase XIV

Manchild throbs-phases,
ALLELUYA!

I Can Say

(from No Baby Must Weep)

i can say
am i not the one who recalls footsteps, hasty, running
on the thick dusty shadows of the night
shadows carrying a frightened little heart on their palms
a red heart
shot in the night in the street for stealing a car
shit like that
getting my children killed
i can say
hurrah 10
i can hear voices and voices and voices
saying child
honey-child
i love you
i can hear voices and voices and voices replying hurrah
and the footsteps have died now
here we are
here we come
one man a million men
come stop here 20
where the footsteps freeze beneath the heels
on this sand
spreading and spreading they say earth becomes earth
here we are now
who will listen
the water is dark
the water is deep
and the water spreads and spreads
and the moon must tumble down . . .
let me seep into africa 30
let this water
this sea
seep into me own me
and break my face into its moods
break my chest
break my heart into its fathoms where no hands reach

let the salt of this sea
settle down like a dove come home, into the wounds that
this earth made in my bosom
ah 40
let this water, this sea
these waves
these colours
this movement
this wide deep blue solid reality break me down like it has rocks
africa

where humility seeps into rocks and roots
singing the heart-breaking tune
africa
harness your cow. . . 50

what is the matter, nothing matters any more
my brother died
folded like a paper wrung by angry hands
and last night a baby came and departed into death
smooth
like a man walking into a door
ah
what's the matter
to belong, to be owned, to be locked
in a million eyes 60
this water
the river the sea
dark
deep
smashing and whistling above the air
choking the bird's whistle

ah
nothing matters any more
nothing

my gait was beaten until it broke like a twig 70
and it is i who heard the laughter
while i choked my cry
i could look into no face they were all bright like the sun

the bone of my heart broke
and the marrow spilled

ah
nothing matters any more
nothing

i can say
i 80
i have gone beyond the flood now
i left the word on the flood
it echoes
in the depth the width
i am beyond the flood

i can say
these eyes
this water this river this flood
washed me
i can say 90
one day the word will break

i can say
one day the laughter will break

i can say
one day the sky will weep
i can say one day
this flower
will stand in the bright bright sun
this flower will have no petals
one day 100

ah
africa
is this not your child come home

When Lights Go Out

(for some who are in South African jails)

I
it is with the shadows of night
when the sun comes and goes
the moon comes and goes
that we ask, in weary voices, which fall into the depth of the gulf:
how does it feel to be you
to be watching and waiting
to feel the heavy weight of every minute come followed by another
and nothing
even everything written in blood
says nothing about how we could wake up tomorrow and build a day 10

II
your eyelids shut, if they ever do,
and the memories of those you knew, flood behind the
darkness of closed eyelids
spiralling into patterns of pain
and you alone know
that once there were hopes
that once the footsteps of the people sounded on the horizon
and now
silence strides across the sky
where the sun sweats, proclaiming a wish to rest

III
can we tell you 20
you the children of a long hour a long day a long night
that hope never befriends fools
yes
time, in absolute eloquence, can erase our faces
remember Sharpeville?
in those days, violence and disaster were articulate
and now
today you watch and wait

IV
so one day hope begins to walk again
it whispers 30
about the twisted corpses that we saw
sprawled across the streets on this knowledgeable earth
the tears
the blood
the memory
and the knowledge, which was born by every heavy minute that we
carried
across a wilderness, where there were no paths
where screams echoed, as if never to stop
it is when there is no hope, that hope begins to walk again
yet 40
like we said
hope never befriends fools

V
since we have eyes to see
ears
and fingers to touch
only if we know how, can we harness time –
can you hear the footsteps

MARTIAL SINDA

Born in 1935 near Brazzaville, Congo Republic. He studied in Brazzaville and Paris and has published one volume of verse: *Premier chant du départ* (Seghers, 1956).

You Will Walk in Peace

You will walk in peace
Through the night,
When you go,
N'dila ho, do not listen
To the voices of the owls
Because
They tell of death.

You will walk in peace.
Through the night
On your way, N'dila ho 10
If you meet a mole
If you smell a certain root
Used when bodies are embalmed
What they foretell is death.

You will sleep in peace
Through the night.
If you hear your name
If you hear a low knock on your door
Never never never answer
For 20
Death is watching you.

You will always be in peace,
O N'dila ho, if you sneeze
During the day;
At night,
Sneezing is an evil sign.

Translated from the French

WOLE SOYINKA

Born in 1934 near Abeokuta, Western Nigeria. He studied in Britain at the University of Leeds and has travelled widely as his reputation as a dramatist has spread. His plays have been performed all over the world, but he has also written poetry as well as essays, novels and autobiographical works. His poetry includes: *Idanre and other poems* (Methuen, 1967); *Poems from Prison* (Rex Collings, 1969); *A Shuttle in the Crypt* (Rex Collings/Methuen, 1972); *Ogun Abibiman* (Rex Collings, 1976).

Telephone Conversation

The price seemed reasonable, location
Indifferent. The landlady swore she lived
Off premises. Nothing remained

But self-confession. 'Madam,' I warned,
'I hate a wasted journey – I am – African.'
Silence. Silenced transmission of
Pressurized good-breeding. Voice, when it came,
Lip-stick coated, long gold-rolled
Cigarette-holder pipped. Caught I was, foully.
'HOW DARK? . . . I had not misheard . . .
'ARE YOU LIGHT 10
OR VERY DARK?' Button B. Button A. Stench
Of rancid breath of public-hide-and-speak.
Red booth. Red pillar-box. Red double-tiered
Omnibus squelching tar. It *was* real! Shamed
By ill-mannered silence, surrender
Pushed dumbfoundment to beg simplification.
Considerate she was, varying the emphasis –
'ARE YOU DARK? OR VERY LIGHT?' Revelation came.
'You mean – like plain or milk chocolate?'
Her assent was clinical, crushing in its light, 20
Impersonality. Rapidly, wave-length adjusted,
I chose, 'West African sepia' – and as an afterthought,
'Down in my passport.' Silence for spectroscopic
Flight of fancy, till truthfulness clanged her accent
Hard on the mouthpiece. 'WHAT'S THAT?' conceding
'DON'T KNOW WHAT THAT IS.' 'Like brunette.'
'THAT'S DARK, ISN'T IT?' 'Not altogether.
'Facially, I am brunette, but madam, you should see
The rest of me. Palm of my hand, soles of my feet
Are a peroxide blond. Friction, caused – 30
Foolishly madam – by sitting down, has turned
My bottom raven black – One moment madam!' – sensing
Her receiver rearing on the thunder clap
About my ears – 'Madam,' I pleaded, 'Wouldn't you rather
See for yourself?'

Koko Oloro

(from a children's propitiation chant)

Dolorous knot
Plead for me
Farm or hill

Plead for me
Stream and wind
Take my voice
Home or road
Plead for me
On this shoot, I
Bind your leaves 10
Stalk and bud
Berries three
On the threshold
Cast my voice
Knot of bitters
Plead for me.

Three Millet Stalks

Three millet
Stalks. A tasselled crown
On a broken glass horizon
Weeds clogged
Their feet, winds came and blew them down

New ears arose
Lean lances through
A stubbed and mangled mound –
And this I saw –
Their grains were ripened closer to the ground. 10

To the Madmen over the Wall

Howl, howl
Your fill and overripeness of the heart,
I may not come with you
Companions of the broken buoy
I may not seek
The harbour of your drifting shore.

Your wise withdrawal
Who can blame? Crouched
Upon your ledge of space, do you witness
Ashes of reality drift strangely past? 10
I fear
Your minds have dared the infinite
And journeyed back
To speak in foreign tongues.

Though walls
May rupture tired seams
Of the magic cloak we share, yet
Closer I may not come
But though I set my ears against
The tune of setting forth, yet, howl 20
Upon the hour of sleep, tell these walls
The human heart may hold
Only so much despair.

JEAN-BAPTISTE TATI-LOUTARD

Born in 1939 at Pointe Noire, Congo Republic. Studied at Bordeaux University in France; he now teaches in Brazzaville. Although he has published a collection of short stories, he is better known as a poet: *Poèmes de la mer* (CLE, 1968); *Les racines congolaises* (P.J. Oswald, 1968); *L'Envers du soleil* (P.J. Oswald, 1970); *Les normes du temps* (Editions du Mont Noir, 1974).

A Woman Speaks

– Summed up in me earth sky and ocean
Birds streams and flowers that you love;
In the pure light of day, you see,
I shine.
I walk towards you, putting aside that octopus
Of night that grips you;
I see you – sad – in the brightness
That uncovers me.

You are transparent to me to the core of your mystery:
You feel stir in me as in the wind 10
The vain ashes of things,
And beauty flare in the sun
Like a scrap of straw;
And man's life sink into the earth
Never to spring again.
You reflect and joy departs;
Come into the only nature where I reach you:
Unremembering let us graze on love,
The only tender grass that grows
Amongst so many hard things. 20
– Woman, you are my lamp. In you I am reflected:
You come to me as a star comes down
Onto the sea;
Ah! why do you not follow the path of the anchor?

Translated from the French

Backside of the Sun

(found upon a man who had killed himself in despair at having betrayed his country)

For a long time I have carried death inside me:
Today, at last, I give it birth.
My journey to the sun terminates here
Among the wreckage of the roads I have run.
The clock of my heart will hang up
on a branch
its rusted pendulum.
In the ancient village, its soul once Portuguese,
They will sing the desperado's hymn
With the disc of a sun already scratched . . . 10
Branch and rope go before me in the wind,
arms dangling.
I pull up my feet from this world
To carry them towards other roads
Nowise of earth.

Translated from the French

Return from Ethiopia

Now I carry inside me so many foreign lands
So many loves passed through in such scattered climes
That at home they think me grown less native to my place.
The last rain fallen drew me back to there
Through the canals of its waters where memory's boat glides,
To a land perched high on the sea and among the ages,
Wheeling its long history on the steed of Menelik.
Ethiopia in September! I glimpse your face
Through colonnades of water where the silhouettes of women are drawn
Who carry your mask imperial which the high wind flourishes; 10
How slender their legs become through excess of noble spirit!
Towards the fields stretch the eucalyptus groves
Perfuming the wretchedness peddled by donkeys at their medieval trot.
The meadows rise and fall at the sun's pleasure
Where the shepherd, forever Abyssinian, sows his songs
Splashed with the lamentation of his flocks.
All this I thought on, by the porthole, hours on end
In the great draw-net of the clouds.

Translated from the French

Crisis of Faith at St Anne's

Rays quartered, the sun turns upside down, in the folds of the clouds.
The rain comes, imposes the noise of its footsteps
And the air as it passes between the railings of water
Turns to rust and sticks to the iron of the posts.
Up there, evening falls with a noise of termites . . .
A shard of moon bends its notched bow against St Anne's
Which raises its antenna at the end of the psalms.
The porch is not far, but in me, faith
Is smashed into tiny memories of piety
On the tortoise-shell of sufferings piled up through the days. 10
My prayer wheels round in the nave, rises up
And dies out in an angle of the ogives.
In the absence of God, through windows that open,
We follow the hazy flight of the clouds.

Translated from the French

TCHICAYA U TAM'SI

Born in 1931 in Mpili, Congo Republic. He went to France in 1946 with his father, who was a Member of Parliament, and he has remained there ever since. He works for UNESCO in Paris. He has written a novel, short stories and plays, but has made his reputation essentially as the most prolific and interesting if most difficult African poet writing in French since Senghor. His poetry includes: *Le Mauvais sang* (Editions Caractères, 1955); *Feu de brousse* (Editions Caractères, 1957); *A triche-coeur* (P.J. Oswald, 1960); *Epitomé* (Société Nationale d'Edition et de Diffusion, Tunis, 1962); *Le Ventre* (Présence Africaine, 1964); *Arc musical* (P.J. Oswald, 1970); *La Veste d'intérieur* (Nubia. 1977). *Selected Poems* (English translations) was published by Heinemann in 1970.

Symbol

A spinning-top turns
What then of its waltz
The child alone watches
The dog comes and barks
The eyes scarcely follow
The frenzy of leaves
A dog comes and barks
O what did you promise?

Can I reach out my hands
Unless for a miracle 10
What then of my waltz
I have shut my eyes
I shall not be present
For my sullen life
The child alone watches
A spinning-top turns

Translated from the French

I Could Say

I could say shit to my life
and leave with my soul in splinters
no one could accuse me of having betrayed
the swallows and the waterfleas
of late derisively my consorts
those hopping time servers
those swooping thieves

But no, I will let my hide and hair
grow old at the stroke of grief
I will not leave until grown old 10
like rum in an oak-cask
my soul dry and brutal
my mouth dry and mocking

Lend me your friend
his pipe or his lip
his lip or his pipe

(let him sleep
tomorrow the hangover
will last until midday)

Translated from the French

Rape

When I had stolen the fire
I promised my blood to the night
for her silence of this crime

But always there came a wine-like dawn
that dissolved my feet
in the nettles of the month of March

I could always
reinvent my fate
with a few aquamarines
picked up on ways once milky 10
now white sands of dry skeletons

A flesh made my flesh sad
A fire liquefied my soul
A wind would have my hands grow porous

A love hardly more pleasant
than the death of the Jew that I order
promises me peace of heart
if I restore the stolen fire
and recover my blood from the night

What did I dare 20
only to put water in my wine
and endure the cold of pebbles
against my lips always
swollen with pain

Translated from the French

Notes on the poems

From the Only Speech That Was Not Delivered at the Rally, *page 1.*
1. *Amanfuo:* in Ashanti, a form of address equivalent to the English 'ladies and gentlemen'

The Place, *page 5.*
This poem and the next were written in Ussher Fort at Accra, 'The Place by the Sea' where the poet was imprisoned in 1975 and held for a year on charges of complicity in a plot to bring about a *coup*. The fort was built originally by the Dutch in the seventeenth century.

One Alone: The Bird Sweeps, *page 6.*
The poem constitutes the fifth and final section of a long poem entitled *The Wayfarer Comes Home.*
28. *gnomic tendencies*: the tendency of tribal societies to enshrine their wisdom in gnomes, that is in versified proverbs or traditional sayings.
39-48. Apparently addressed, like parts of the earlier sections of the poem, to the poet's wife.
56. *an ancient stool*: chieftaincy.
68. *Soweto*: name of the huge African township near Johannesburg (shortened form of South Western Townships) where the student protests of 1976 were going on at the time the poem was written.

On the Island, *page 9.*
'The Island' is Robben Island, a few miles off Cape Town, where black political prisoners are detained. A number of poems by South African poets take the island as their theme for it has become a powerful symbol of the repression of apartheid. These poems contain many of the associations that accompany the image of the prison – confinement and loss of freedom (barbed wire fences), hard labour (work in the quarry), sexual abuse and, heightened by the island image, the themes of isolation, separation and exile.

It Was a Sherded World I Entered, *page 12.*
sherded: from *sherd* (more usually *shard*), a piece of broken pottery.

Robben Island Sequence, *page 12.*
Robben Island: see note on 'On the Island', *page 9.*
36. *Kleynhans:* the Afrikaans name of a prison guard.

58. *old lags*: those who have been in prison for some time and have been placed in charge of groups of prisoners working in the rock quarries.
61. *span*: an Afrikaans word for a team of oxen hitched to a wagon, also used as here for a gang of workers.

Looking for the Spirit at Night, *page 15.*
16. *Manfred*: the poet's dead brother.

You May Well Cry, *page 16.*
A speech from the close of John Pepper Clark's play, *The Song of a Goat.* It is a comment on the deaths of the main characters which have just occurred, and on the difficulty of understanding the meaning of the tragedy.
7. *for laugh*: 'for laughter'.

Night Rain, *page 16.*
10. *Droning with insistent ardour upon . . .*: rain is falling upon the roof, and the water is coming in through the sheaves of the thatch which are thin enough for the flashes of lightning to be seen through them. The water drips past the roof rafters underneath, which it is too dark for the poet to see clearly.
19. *Much like beads I could in prayer tell*: the drops of water falling into the bowls set to catch them could be used by the poet like the beads of a rosary, for counting his prayers.

Ibadan, *page 18.*
The rusting corrugated iron roofs of this huge Nigerian city cover many square miles.

Incident at the Police Station, Warri, *page 18.*
The Flagellation of Jesus by Piero della Francesca: the fifteenth-century Italian painter Piero della Francesca shows in a famous picture the scourging of Jesus (Mark 15.15, etc.) taking place before Pilate in an elegant marble hall. Jesus stands beside a soldier with a raised whip but there is no attempt to depict violence or suffering. Almost half the picture space is taken up by three figures in the foreground, grouped in conversation, apparently unconcerned or unaware of what is taking place behind them. There is in the picture nothing to correspond to the car and the last two lines of the poem but the use of the word *gallant* and the reference to wine and song are perhaps meant to suggest Renaissance Italy.

The Casualties, *page 19.*
The casualties are those of the Nigerian civil war.

The Lagos-Ibadan Road before Shagamu, *page 20.*
The 'legends' given in capital letters are mottoes of the kind commonly painted on the buses in Nigeria.

The Lines of Our Hands, *page 21.*
5. *Homeric fights*: battles between great heroes such as are described in the poetry of the ancient Greek poet Homer.

The Rock behind the Fort, *page 23.*
See note to 'The Place', *page 5*

Viaticum, *page 25.*
'Viaticum' originally meant the preparations and provisions for a journey (here, the journey of life). In the Catholic Church it is the name for the Communion given to a person in danger of death as preparation for the journey to the next life. The poet uses this word with strong Christian associations as the title of a poem about a traditional African ceremony which assures him the protective presence of his ancestors throughout his life.

Breath, *page 26.*
47-49. *. . . our fate is bound to the law,*
And the fate of the dead who are not dead
To the spirits of breath who are stronger than they.
The life of man is bound to the life of nature because nature is full of the spirits of the human dead, and these in turn are bound to what the poet calls the spirits of breath, the spirit of nature itself.

My Brother and I Left the Apartment, *page 31.*
The poem given is the latter part of a verse narrative which describes the poet's return to Paris after a brief stay in Morocco and Spain in 1968.

Schoolboys, *page 33.*
13. *Homer's company*; 14. *Eluard's poems and Perrault's tales*: the schoolboy goes to school to absorb the culture of Europe here typified by the ancient Greek poet Homer, the twentieth-century French poet Paul Eluard and the old French folk tales as rewritten and adapted to the taste of his time by Charles Perrault at the end of the seventeenth century.
15. *Kotje*: Kotje-Barma, a philosopher and moralist of the seventeenth century, hero of many stories in Wolof oral tradition.

A Heritage of Liberation, *page 37.*
The poet speaks on behalf of his own generation as it comes to its end and bequeaths to its descendants the ideal of freedom which has inspired it. The quest for freedom is seen in terms of a battle, with its association not only with 'weapons' but also suffering, bloodshed and death. The poem ends with the image of a new day about to begin, bringing nearer perhaps the final achievement of liberation.

Pigeons at the Oppenheimer Park, *page 43.*
1. *Oppenheimer Park*: a public park in Johannesburg.
6. *Separate Amenities Act*: a South African law which makes it obligatory to provide separate public facilities for blacks and whites – including separate park benches. It is illegal to sit on a bench not intended for your race.
13. *Holy Ideology!*: a satirical reference to the 'holy ideology' of apartheid, which its promoters endow with the force of divine law, but here used as a

profane exclamation modelled on such phrases as 'holy mackerel!' used in comics.

13–14. . . . *those two at the crest*
of the jumping impala . . .

There is a large piece of sculpture in the park in the form of a whole arching herd of leaping impala (a kind of deer).

17. *Immorality Act*: a South African law that forbids sexual relations or marriage between people of different colours; *Sies!*: a very commonly used Afrikaans expression of disgust.

Amagoduka at Glencoe Station, *page 46.*

Amagoduka: Zulu mine labour recruits.

2. *Vryheid*; 3. *Blood River*; 7. *Dundee; 11. Glencoe*: the train carrying the *amagoduka* is on its way from Zululand to *EGoli* (line 73: 'gold', the popular African name for Johannesburg, where South Africa's gold is mined). Starting at Vryheid, it crosses Blood River, named after a famous battle in which the Boers defeated the Zulus in 1838, and stops at the coalmining towns of Dundee and Glencoe. Since the train then goes on to the coastal city of *Durban* (line 15), the *amagoduka* must change at Glencoe, where they will catch a train to take them inland to Johannesburg.

19. *'non-European Males' waiting room*: see note on the Separate Amenities Act given under 'Pigeons at the Oppenheimer Park', *page 43.*

30. *mqombothi*: a Zulu beer.

51. *Msinga*: a town in the mountainous part of Natal province.

72. *Tugela river*: the river that separates Zululand from the rest of Natal province.

Song for a Passport, *page 53.*

The poet is determined to leave South Africa although it means the end of a love affair and although he knows he may have difficulties, being non-white, in persuading the authorities to issue him with a passport. In the first part of the poem he is reflecting while shaving on the morning when he must present himself for interview; in the second part, he is in the waiting room ready to be called. Abandoned girl friend and the South African state are identified in their reluctance to let him go, but he is determined to win free of both.

20. *the dull green voucher*; 23. *gold lettering*: the South African passport has a dark green cover and gold lettering.

Letter from Pretoria Central Prison, *page 54.*

This poem is not based on personal experience as, unlike Dennis Brutus, Nortje was not himself ever imprisoned in South Africa.

29. *double feature*: two feature films making up a single programme.

Native's Letter, *page 55.*

14. *Tshaka*: more usually spelt Chaka or Shaka; the creator of the Zulu nation and a brilliant general. He was born c. 1787 and was assassinated in 1828 by

his brother Dingane. *Hendrik Witbooi*: lived *c.* 1840–1905; he was the leader of a Khokhoi tribe who were the original inhabitants of the Cape, later settling in what is now Namibia. He actively resisted German colonization in the area in the early 1890s. *Adam Kok*: lived *c.* 1810–75; ruler of the Griquas (composed of descendants of the Khokhoi people who originally lived around Cape Town) who had settled in the western part of the Cape Province in the early eighteenth century. Adam Kok came into conflict with the Boers as they too moved away from Cape Town in the 1830s and 1840s in search of land.
15. *Xhosa*: the first Africans to come into contact with the whites as they moved towards one another along the eastern portion of the Cape in the late eighteenth century. Conflict continued throughout much of the nineteenth century; the Xhosa believed that one day they would drive the white man into the sea.
16. *moonlights*: to moonlight is to work secretly (usually at night) at a second job in order to earn enough to live on; here it refers to the way Africans have to leave the real job of farming their land to go to Johannesburg and earn money on the gold mines in order to feed and clothe their families.
26. *Karsh*: a famous photographer.
27. *siberia*: a common noun derived from Siberia, in Russia, where people are sent as a punishment to work in the salt mines.

All Hungers Pass Away, *page 57.*
Nortje left South Africa in 1965 and studied in England and Canada. This poem – his last – was written on his return to Oxford from Canada in September 1970. It evokes his depressed state of mind at the time.
18. *sherry circuit*: the round of sherry parties that constitutes the basis of social life in the English academic community.
19. *Drakensberg*: the Drakensberg mountain range is the longest, highest and most spectacular in South Africa.

Were I to Choose, *page 58.*
A poem written in a style owing much to that of the Welsh poet Dylan Thomas. The poet considers how he was conceived in the womb, how his crying as a new-born child stands for the griefs of his future years. Now, at thirty-one years, his thoughts are confused and only death brings calm. Neither to be born nor to die is in our choice.
21. *harmattan*: a hot, dry wind in West Africa that blows from the Sahara Desert from December to February.

One Night at Victoria Beach, *page 60.*
4. *Aladuras'*: the Aladuras are members of a Yoruba Christian sect with great belief in the power of prayer. The name comes from the Yoruba word *adura*, meaning 'prayer'.
8. *highlife*: a kind of dance music popular in Nigeria.
10. *washer-words*: the rubber washer binds the two metal parts of a tap together,

just as words bind lovers or buyers and sellers.
25. *Babalawo*: a Yoruba traditional diviner.

For Georgette, *page 62.*
2. *The newcomer:* the poet's newly-born niece.

Come Thunder, *page 62.*
The title has the sense 'Let the thunder come' and the poem foretells, even invokes, some huge catastrophe to come as a retribution and consummation for the corruption and disintegration of Nigerian society.

Hurrah for Thunder, *page 63.*
The poet's enthusiasm for the thunder in this poem becomes more outspoken – dangerously so, as he indicates in the closing couplet.
3. *tetrarch of the jungle*: the Herod in the New Testament who put John the Baptist to death is called 'the tetrarch'; hence any ruthless and arbitrary ruler. The word itself means 'ruler of four', i.e. the fourth part of a Roman province, and the poet plays on this in lines 5 and 6.

Elegy for Alto, *page 64.*
Mourning song to be sung in a high voice – or perhaps played on the alto-horn. In this poem, the disaster the poet foretold has struck and now he pleads for release from his poetic office. The eagle was the bird of the Roman god of thunder and the thunderbolt, Jupiter, and the image carried on the standards of the Roman army. Robbers and politicians become interchangeable as the poem progresses. Lines 17–20 seem to allude to the story of Abraham and Isaac (Genesis 22) and the concluding four lines are possibly suggested by Acts 1.11.

The Song of Lawino, *page 65.*
'I am not unfair to my husband' and 'Time Has Become' are extracts from Okot p'Bitek's long poem *The Song of Lawino.* Ocol, Lawino's husband, has abandoned her for a westernized woman, and the poem is a long monologue in which Lawino attacks him for turning from her and the traditional ways of their people.

Time Has Become, *page 68.*
16. *Acoli*: pronounced and usually written Acholi, the name of the Ugandan people to whom Okot p'Bitek belongs and of the language in which this poem was originally written.

You Talk to Me of 'Self', *page 73.*
7. *mascara*: a black-coloured cosmetic to beautify the eyelashes.

All Day Long, *page 75.*
3. *Cayor and Baol*: provinces of Senegal.
7. *Sine*: province of Senegal from which Senghor comes.

Taga for Mbaye Dyob, *page 76.*
taga: lament.
tama: a small drum used by griots (see note to line 16), carried under the arm.
11. *rivers of the South*: the rivers of Casamance, a very picturesque region in southern Senegal.
16. *griots*: in Senegal, troubadour poets and actors, once retained by noble families to sing their praises and genealogies; they enjoyed the right to criticize freely. ('Griot' is pronounced 'gree-o'.)
22. *from Ngabu to the Walo, from Ngalam to the sea*: Ngabu and Ngalam are inland in Senegal, and the Walo is the name of a region on the banks of the Senegal River near the coast. The poet emphasizes that the songs of the young girls will be heard throughout the country.
23. *kora*: a type of harp in Senegal.

Ndessé, *page 77.*
Ndessé: a Serer word meaning sadness, 'the blues'.
2. *gymnic feast*: a reference to the wrestling matches held among the Serers of Senegal.
4. *Kor-Sanou;* exclamation meaning: 'champion of Sanou'; *Katamague*: the coast to the south of Dakar where Senghor was born.
10. *As when good Serer women* . . .: Senghor writes in one of his essays: 'I remember my Serer grandmothers used to have recourse to God in times of great distress. They would dress like men, with all the trappings, fire guns and shoot arrows into the air. They would even go so far as to use vulgar language in French.'
11. *paragnessé*: a popular Serer corruption of the word *français*, French.
15. *marabout*: Muslim religious teacher. It is customary in West Africa for parents to give their children into his care for their religious education. These are the disciples referred to.

Message, *page 79.*
9. *the tribes that let fly a poisonous greeting*: i.e. who shoot poisonous arrows or darts at strangers.
13. *kailcedrats*: the kailcedrat is a shady tree found in Senegal.
15. *Elissa*: place in northern Guinea-Bissau from which Senghor's family originally came.
22. *You decline the rose*: a reference to the learning of Latin, where *rosa* is used in grammar books as the model for the first declension of nouns; *your ancestors are the Gauls:* a French history text-book, formerly used in primary schools in French West Africa, began with a reference to *our ancestors the Gauls.*
23. *Sorbonne*: the original name for the oldest part of the University of Paris.
24. *golden louis*: gold coins of the reign of the French King Louis XIV.
30. *Mbissel*; *Fa'oy*: two pagan shrines near Senghor's birthplace.
41. *ivory message*: a reference to the carved ivory staff carried by a chief's messenger when he bears a message to another chief.

And the Sun, *page 81.*
9. *Cap de Nase*: cliffs not far from Dakar; *Mamelles*: two volcanic hills near Dakar (*mamelles* is French for 'breasts') – the lighthouse is built on one of them.

A Ballad on the Thing, *page 83.*
'The Thing' is the poet's pass which, like all Africans in South Africa, he is obliged to carry at all times. If he does not have it on him, he is likely to be arrested. 'The man' is a policeman – armed (stanza 8), as white policemen are in South Africa. The arrival of 'a brother' – another African – (stanza 12) gives the poet confidence to brazen out the situation instead of running away; this stanza is probably intended to suggest, more generally, that the black people of South Africa should confront white repression together.

The Island, *page 85.*
The Island: see note to 'On the Island' by Dennis Brutus, *page 9.*
20. *[Nelson] Mandela:* a leader of the African National Congress of South Africa, sentenced to life imprisonment on Robben Island in 1963; *[Walter] Sisulu:* a leader of the African National Congress. He was sentenced to life imprisonment on Robben Island in 1964.

Words, Words, Words, *page 86.*
The poet is criticizing the way the current jargon of apartheid seeks to hide the repressive nature of its policies and the hypocrisy of its claims to be offering South African blacks their freedom in creating the so-called 'homelands'. Words like 'nations', 'homeland', 'independence' and 'bloodless revolution' do not describe the reality of the blackman's situation in South Africa.

For Don M. – Banned, *page 88.*
Don M.: Don Mattera, the South African poet, who was until recently banned by the authorities. In South Africa, a banned person may not attend meetings or social gatherings, he may not travel outside a fixed radius from his place of residence, and neither he nor anyone else may publish anything he writes.

Ofay-Watcher, Throbs-Phase, *page 88.*
Ofay-watcher: ofay is a black American term for 'whiteman'.
Throbs-phase: the poem is divided into stanzas, or sections ('phases'), reflecting the throbbing of the poet's heart.
35. *haai:* an exclamation – 'look here!'
65. *Park Station:* the railway station in Johannesburg where the African workers begin their journey back to Soweto after their day's work in the white city. (For Soweto, see 'One Alone: The Bird Sweeps', *page 6.*)
77. *8th Avenue:* a street in Soweto.

I Can Say, *page 92.*
This is the concluding section of Serote's long poem *No Baby Must Weep.*

When Lights Go Out, *page 95.*
25. *Sharpeville:* in 1960, the police fired on a crowd of demonstrators in the township of Sharpeville in South Africa, killing 67 people and wounding 186. The demonstrators, who had offered no provocation towards the police, were shot as they fled. The incident caused a sense of shock throughout the world and has become a symbol of South African repression.

Telephone Conversation, *page 97.*
11. *Button B Button A:* at the time when the poem was written coin-telephones in Britain had two buttons, one marked A, to make connection, the other marked B which could be pressed to retrieve the coins if the number was engaged or unobtainable. The poet in his embarrassment stares about him, at the telephone controls, at the public telephone box from which he is calling; at a post office pillar box, at a passing bus.
23–4. *spectroscopic/Flight of fancy:* consideration or an analysis in the mind of a range of shades of colour.

Koko Oloro, *page 98.*
15. *Knot of bitters:* tied bunch of bitter or medicinal herbs.

Three Millet Stalks, *page 99.*
This poem and the next arise from the poet's period of imprisonment by the Federal authorities during the civil war.

To the Madmen over the Wall, *page 99.*
Soyinka was imprisoned in Kaduna in a set of buildings where lunatics were also confined.
4. *Companions of the broken buoy:* the madmen are adrift with nothing left to mark their course.
17. *The magic cloak we share:* poet and madmen have the magic power to wrap themselves up from reality and escape by means of the imagination. But it is not the same for both – the cloak is not seamless. The poet is duty-bound to resist the escape into madness himself.

Return from Ethiopia, *page 102.*
7. *Menelik:* emperor of Ethiopia from 1889 to 1913; he successfully resisted the Italian attempt to conquer the country and laid the foundations for its modern administration.
15. *Abyssinian:* Abyssinia is another name for Ethiopia.

Crisis of Faith at St Anne's, *page 102.*
St Anne's: The Roman Catholic cathedral in Brazzaville, Congo Republic.
12. *ogives:* arches.

Rape, *page 104.*
1. *When I had stolen the fire:* the poet likens himself to Prometheus, the Greek demi-god who stole fire from the gods to give it to man.
16. *the Jew:* Christ.

Further reading

Poems of Black Africa, edited by Wole Soyinka (Heinemann, 1975), is a large and wide-ranging selection of poems in English or translated from African languages, French and Portuguese. An interesting feature of this collection is the arrangement of the poems according to theme.

Modern Poetry from Africa, edited by Gerald Moore and Ulli Beier (Penguin, revised edition, 1968) is a well-established and respected anthology covering the whole range of African poetry, although published too long ago now to take account of the new poetry from South Africa.

French African Verse, edited by John Reed and Clive Wake (Heinemann, 1972), is a representative collection of poetry from French-speaking Africa. The original French texts are accompanied by verse translations and there is a full bibliography.

Messages: Poems from Ghana, edited by Kofi Awoonor and G. Adali-Mortty (Heinemann, 1971), contains a selection of the poetry of twelve Ghanaian poets.

There are several anthologies of South African poetry. Three particularly useful ones are: *Seven South African Poets*, edited by Cosmo Pieterse (Heinemann, 1971); *Black Poets in South Africa*, edited by Robert Royston (Heinemann, 1973); *Poets to the People, South African Freedom Poems*, edited by Barry Feinberg (Heinemann, 1980).